THE GAME OF DOUBLES

IN TENNIS

The Game of

Diagrams by STEPHEN P. BALDWIN

Doubles in Tennis

by

WILLIAM F. TALBERT and BRUCE S. OLD

J. B. LIPPINCOTT COMPANY

Philadelphia · New York

To

NANCY *and* BUNNY

Foreword

The singles and doubles games of lawn tennis are different in many respects. The singles game is a purely individual one, whereas the doubles game is a team game in which both players must study each other's play and learn to combine if they wish to succeed.

Bill Talbert, who has written this book together with Bruce Old, was a great player in his time—and his time was not so long ago. Now, as Captain of the United States Davis Cup team, he is charged not only with the selection and alignment of his forces but also with spotting and helping to bring along the young players who one day may make the team. To my mind it is entirely fitting that his experience with and understanding of the game should now be preserved in the first book devoted exclusively to the technique of doubles play.

The Game of Doubles in Tennis deals with the many practical and theoretic differences between singles and doubles play. It examines thoroughly the vital return of service, the volley, net play, the lob, anticipation, base-line play (which we are advised—properly—to avoid whenever possible), teamwork, and all the other elements that go into the making of successful doubles teams. It illustrates with many simple diagrams the ways and means by which great players carried out their "doubles thinking." It contains pictures of past and present doubles champions, pictures and diagrams of key tournament points. In a word, it is a storehouse of doubles information and a valuable aid to the aspiring player.

I welcome it and commend it to all lovers of the game.

—*Sir Norman Brookes*

Contents

THE GAME OF DOUBLES

IN TENNIS

Introduction

This is the first book ever written on the game of doubles in tennis. To bear this bouncing baby has taken seven long years of hard labor. The Library of Congress and the Boston, New York, and Cleveland Public Libraries were researched from top to bottom. Then data were assembled on numerous matches in order that facts, not mere impressions, could be presented.

It is the fond hope of the authors that this book will enhance your enjoyment of playing and watching this great game of doubles. Perhaps it may help win you a tennis title one of these days. It would be fantastic to suppose that it might help the United States win the Davis Cup some year—but, at least, we can dream about that.

In doubles, strategy and tactics are as important as stroke production. To present more clearly some of the plays and positions, the text is supplemented with many diagrams. A list of symbols, on the following page, helps the reader to follow the plays.

A complete play, diagramed in Figure 1, shows a sequence of shots that happens all too often and may be classified as one of the cardinal sins of week-end doubles players. Like most sins, this one is not new, having been pointed out by numerous writers as early as 1900; it is committed even today with amazing regularity. The sinner is the server, player **A**. What should player **A** have done? The answer to that and many other questions may be found in the following pages.

While there is not one book on doubles, many volumes may be found in almost any public library on the mechanics of stroke production in tennis. For this reason no attempt will be made to cover this subject in this book.

A Solid oval denotes tennis player, and letter identifies the player.

Dotted line shows the path of player moving from one position to another, the arrow indicating direction.

Solid line shows flight of tennis ball, the arrow indicating direction.

Dash-dot line shows a lob.

Small circle shows bounce point of ball.

Large circle shows aim point for a shot.

Circle with star shows aim point for a placement.

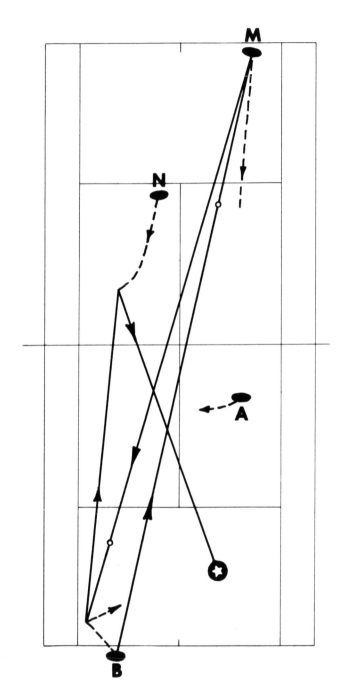

Figure 1

Player **B** serves to receiver **M** and then commits his first and most serious mistake: he fails to move in to the net position following his serve. Receiver **M** takes advantage of this by hitting a deep return and following his shot into the net position, thus taking the offensive away from the serving team. In returning the ball server **B** makes his second mistake by hitting his shot down the line to player **N**, who has moved in to the net position. The faulty tactics of the serving team are now evident. Player **N** notes that the whole diagonal area of the court is open to him. All he has to do is move a couple of steps and hit an easy cross-court volley at the aim point shown to make a placement and win the point. While player **B** has made not a single error, he has committed two tactical mistakes which have resulted in making his team look foolish as well as losing the point.

But why a special book on doubles?

Doubles is not just singles with two players on each side of the net instead of one. It is, to quote Helen Wills, "a game entirely by itself." Yet, to date there never has been a book on doubles. Since about half of all tennis played is doubles, the first book is long overdue. The lack of a book on the fundamentals of doubles has hurt the development of the game. In the United States today tennis players normally do not start to grasp the fine points of doubles until they reach the age of about thirty-five. There are two reasons for this: people in this age group start to play more doubles than singles, and they also start to think more about the game. Then suddenly it happens! With a bang they wake up to the fact that doubles is really a better game than singles or any other sport you may care to mention. Then they regret that this realization did not come to them earlier, because of the fun they have missed, and the superior strokes and techniques they might have developed, had they started sooner.

Just think, maybe you could have been a champion! If not an international champion, at least the town or club or summer resort or school or camp champion. Yes, if only you had started playing sooner and had learned something about the game. That little word "if" has been called the saddest word in any language. Well, this book, it is hoped, will eliminate the "if" by giving you the inspiration to play and the knowledge to enjoy good doubles. Yes, instead of a could-have-been champion perhaps you will get that extra lift to win a silver cup. Who knows, you might even play Davis Cup or Wightman Cup doubles some day!

It is always interesting, and sometimes convincing, for players young and old to hear what some of the masters think about a game. Let's take a look at some typical quotations.

Vincent Richards has this to say of the game of doubles: "Nothing is more spectacular than a first-class doubles match; even more than singles play, the doubles game provides a test of generalship and resourcefulness that challenges the utmost concentration and ingenuity of the player." Some ardent admirers of the game of singles may consider this opinion to be slightly prejudiced, since Richards was a tennis standout largely in doubles. However, some of the best singles players in history go even further in their praise of doubles:

J. DONALD BUDGE: "For sheer enjoyment, thrills, and satisfaction you can't beat a good game of doubles between two evenly matched teams of the first rank. There is more fun in doubles, both for the players and the spectators."

FRED PERRY: "Certainly I agree that the four-handed game, well played, is the art of lawn tennis at its highest."

BILL TILDEN: "Singles is a game of imagination, doubles is a game of exact angles."

RENE LACOSTE: "It is owing to modern ideas on court position in doubles that a doubles match is often considered more attractive, more amusing, and more varied than a singles match."

MAURICE McLOUGHLIN: "I venture to say that doubles requires a greater variety of strokes . . ."

This book is aimed at improving doubles play for the international star or the week-end player or the rawest beginner. It covers the history of the game, the over-all framework of doubles, the serve, return of service, net play, base line play and, finally, a summary. Stroke production, as we have said, will not be discussed because many excellent, well-illustrated books have already been written on the subject. Since doubles is a game of complex tactics and teamwork, a study of it must go into what may seem at first to be great detail. But the rewards for following this detail are great. With application your game should improve by "fifteen" and your enjoyment by "thirty." You will not commit obvious mistakes; your partner will no longer glare at you; and the rallies will be more prolonged and exciting. Even if you and your partner are tired old businessmen, you can make two dashing young club singles finalists look a little ridiculous at the game. Yes, this troubled world will truly become a sunnier spot.

To whet your appetite one final bit, we decided to select for your pleasure the dream doubles team of all time.

Our choice is George M. Lott, Jr., of the United States or John E. Bromwich of Australia as the top tactician, and J. Donald Budge or John A. Kramer of the United States as the top power player. Lott and Bromwich were the great masters of the game of doubles. They were primarily play makers. In other words they utilized thought, study, court craft, stroke variety, finesse, spin, tactics, fakes, teasers, anticipation, and well-planned maneuvers to force the opponents either into making a weak return or leaving an opening. All these masters needed as a partner to make a dream team was a rangy, power player to take maximum advantage of every opening they established. And no two players ever walked on a doubles court who could match the combination of pulverizing power and sound doubles play of Budge and Kramer. Their devastating forehands and overheads permitted them to put away almost anything, and their famous backhands made them equally overpowering on that side. With two years of practice and play together to develop all-important teamwork this dream combination would have been unbeatable.

Upon being notified of their selection, these four great players kindly submitted brief comments on the game. The wisdom of their remarks will become more apparent as you proceed into the chapters which follow.

"To choose the perfect, or dream doubles player, there are, of course, many things to look for. However, after giving it much thought, these are the requirements that I would prefer.

"It goes without saying that this player must possess all of the basic shots, and perhaps excel in a few. He would forget all about trying to serve aces except for rare occasions, and concentrate on getting his first serve in as consistently as possible. He would at all times play his volleys deep and down the center, using the alleys only when they were wide open, but even then hating himself whilst doing so. (However, the only time deep volleys wouldn't be logical would be if the four players were in at the net; then a short or low shot at the opponent's feet is the answer until you get the one you want to put away.) He should be able to play defensively as well as offensively. And he should have the type of personality that encourages talk during the match: there is nothing worse to me than having a doubles partner that won't 'talk it up.' There are always times when things aren't going well in almost any match, and if you can talk about these with your partner in an honest way, you can usually circumvent them."

—J. DONALD BUDGE.

"As a first court doubles player, I feel that to achieve success it is most essential for the player to understand the value of service returns which he must make with regular consistency.

"Returning-of-service is so important, and ability to appreciate the strength of your opponents against varying returns is essential.

"The receiver must be able to make long- or short-angled returns or center court shots; and above all he should lob occasionally with controlled disguise.

"For best results the ball should be taken on the rise and played low and quickly over the net, enabling both yourself and partner to gain an offensive position at the net before the server can make the close volleying area.

"The player in the first court should endeavor to win the first point of each service, enabling his partner to try to force home the advantage and thus effect a breakthrough.

"He should be content to work for openings, be consistent with his return and prepared to forsake spectacular play in the best interests of developing teamwork and understanding with his partner.

"A sound tip in doubles: do not play an angle unless you can make a sure placement. An angle shot is a risk, so why take unnecessary risks? When in doubt, low down the center is the safest method of gaining success."

—JOHN E. BROMWICH.

"In commenting on the qualifications for the ideal doubles player, I would like to emphasize a factor which is all too often overlooked. Others have pointed out the importance of various strokes, maintaining the offensive, etc. I want to stress anticipation. The thing which separates the great from the near-great doubles players is the uncanny ability to anticipate the actions of their opponents. This art is not well understood by the average doubles player, especially the youngsters. But it is something which can and should be developed through thought and practice.

"There are four parts to anticipation. The first is in the placing of your own shot. Suppose you and your partner are at net, and your opponents have one man at net, and one on his way in to net. You hit a volley near the middle of the court that bounces at the service line, so that the advancing opponent must get set to play a ground stroke from that point. By placing your volley there you have taken the first step in anticipating the return because you should know what to look for. In this instance you should look for one of three types of returns—a drive down the center, a dink at your feet, or a well-hidden lob hit over the longest dimension of the court.

"The second is in developing knowledge of the method of stroking and types of strokes most used by the opponent about to strike the ball. This involves learning the give-away motions of stroke production, idiosyncrasies, habits, and favorite shots of the opponents under certain tactical conditions.

"The third is in concentrating on the motions of the opponent as he is in the act of striking the ball. You should watch the position of his feet, body, arm, backswing, and racquet. These details may appear to be complicated, but after practice they can be noted at a glance. In this way you can detect which one of the three shots he intends to make.

"The fourth and final thing is for you and your partner to shift position to meet the by-now well-anticipated return. This move can not be started too soon as it might permit the opponent to change his mind.

"Yes sir, give me a parner with the 'feel' of anticipation and he will have made a long stride toward being the dream doubles player."

—JOHN A. KRAMER.

"The successful doubles player, to my way of thinking, must have, in addition to the fundamentals such as putting the first serve in play, a three-way choice of shots from the back court. As we know, doubles is mainly a matter of getting a service break, and then hanging on for dear life. Therefore, it behooves us to devise ways and means to obtain that service break.

"One way, of course, is through sheer power, but so few of us are able to do that that it is necessary to rely on cunning and cleverness. I suggest that, like a baseball pitcher who throws his fast ball, curve, and change-of-pace ball, all with the same motion, the tennis player learn to make a forehand drive, a lob, and a soft, tantalizing shot, as the baseball pitcher, with the same motion. With control, and these three shots well disguised, he will find it considerably easier to dislodge his opponents from the advantageous net position."

—GEORGE M. LOTT, JR.

And so, now you have a devastating team to dream about emulating! Ah, sweet dreams!

CHAPTER II

History

It all started in England in 1873. That was the year lawn tennis was invented by Major Walter Clopton Wingfield. A description of the game was first recorded for some of his friends in a booklet, *The Major's Game of Lawn Tennis*—dedicated to the party assembled at Nantclwyd in December, 1873. His interesting summary of the game is well worth quoting:

"The Game of Tennis may be traced back to the days of the ancient Greeks, under the name of σφαιριστικὴ. It was subsequently played by the Romans under the name of 'Pila.' It was the fashionable pastime of the nobles of France, during the reign of Charles V, and it was in vogue in England as early as Henry III, and is described by Gregory as 'one of the most ancient games in Christendom.' 'Henry V,' 'Henry VII,' and Henry VIII were all tennis players, and it has only now died out owing to the difficulties of the game, and the expense of erecting courts. All these difficulties have been surmounted by the inventor of 'Lawn Tennis,' which has all the interest of 'tennis,' and has the advantage that it may be played in the open air in any weather by people of any age and both sexes. In a hard frost the nets may be erected on the ice, and the players being equipped with skates, the Game assumes a new feature, and gives an opening for the exhibition of much grace and science.

"Croquet, which of late years has monopolized the attention of the public, lacks the healthy and manly excitement of 'Lawn Tennis.' Moreover, this game has the advantage that, while an adept at tennis or racquets would rapidly become a really scientific player, the merest tyro can learn it in five minutes sufficiently well for all practical purposes."

Wingfield could not resist adding some advice: "Hit your ball gently, and look well before striking, so as to place it in the corner most remote from your adversary. A great deal of side can be imparted to the ball by the proper touch, which, together with a nice appreciation of strength, adds much to the delicacy and science of the game."

Major Wingfield applied for a patent on the game February 23, 1874, and was awarded Letters Patent No. 685 for "A Portable Court for Playing Tennis." The game became popular the world over quite rapidly, largely because of its enthusiastic adoption by the British Army as a barracks exercise.

Tennis was brought to the United States by a lady, bless her soul. In the spring of 1874 Miss Mary Outerbridge argued strenuously to get through the U. S. Customs Service some strange-looking equipment she had acquired from some British Army officers in Bermuda. This equipment turned out to be what she needed to set up a private tennis court on Staten Island in order to introduce the game to the United States. Permission was granted her to build the court on the grounds of the Staten Island Cricket and Baseball Club at Camp Washington. The following year at Nahant, Massachusetts, two players named Dr. James Dwight, destined to become one of the early doubles tennis champions, and Mr. F. R. Sears, Jr., started to popularize the game by playing in public places.

Tennis was introduced in India in 1875; Germany in 1876; France in 1877; and Australia in 1878.

The first doubles championship tournament was played at Wimbledon, England, in 1879. After some seventy-five years the game of doubles in tennis is finally coming into its deserved spot in the sun. It has emerged completely from the doldrums of 1895, when its rating as a spectator sport was indeed low. Championship doubles has now been developed to the point where varied, fast, smashing, technically superior team play usually makes it more interesting, exciting, and amusing for the gallery than topflight singles. And in the tennis clubs around the world it is more popular than singles.

The three most important doubles encounters each year are the final rounds of the United States National Doubles Championship, the United Kingdom Wimbledon Tournament, and the Davis Cup Challenge Round. Their histories are replete with the famous names of men, and women too, who have brought the game to its present great heights. The Wimbledon tournament is the oldest of the three, having been held every year since 1879, except for wartime interruptions. The

United States Lawn Tennis Association inaugurated the National Doubles Championship Tournament in 1881. It has been played every year since then, although the form of the tournament was altered somewhat during certain war years. In 1900 Dwight F. Davis, one of the famous early tennis players in the United States, donated the Davis Cup for competition between nations to determine world supremacy in tennis.

TABLE I

DAVIS CUP CHALLENGE ROUNDS

Nation	No. of Challenge Rounds	No. of Challenge Rounds Won	No. of Doubles Matches Won	Percentage of Doubles Matches Won
U.S.	43	19	20	47
Australia	35	21	23	66
Great Britain ..	16	9	7	44
France	9	6	4	44
Italy	2	0	0	0
Japan	1	0	0	0
Belgium	1	0	0	0
Mexico	1	0	0	0
Spain	1	0	0	0
India	1	0	1	100

This famous Cup has now been won fifty-five times and has been responsible for increased interest in tennis the world over. Incidentally, Mr. Davis was himself a United States, Wimbledon, and Davis Cup doubles champion.

The Davis Cup Challenge Round consists of five matches played in three days. The first and third days are devoted to singles play, two matches being played each day. The second day is reserved for the famous doubles encounter. Of the fifty-five Davis Cup Challenge Rounds played through 1966, eleven were won by a three-to-two score because of a victory in doubles. Numerous other doubles victories have no doubt contributed the deciding point because of the big psychological advantage afforded by a two-to-one lead after a split in the opening day's singles matches. It is these Davis Cup struggles that have contributed more than any one thing to the development of the present-day spectacular type of doubles game. Of special interest is the fact that the Australians, as shown in Table I, have by far the best record for Davis Cup doubles play. Six of the eleven Challenge Rounds won by a doubles victory have been annexed by the smart, fighting Aussies.

The most famous doubles players of history and their records, selected on the basis of their deeds in the three most important tournaments, are listed in Tables II and III. The outstanding players are named in the left-hand column and their several partners in the right-hand column to help the reader compare individual records. Several well-known players, whose winning streaks were not extended over a sufficiently long period, have necessarily been omitted. And it is sad

TABLE II

Name and Nationality	Tournament and Year of Victory		
	Wimbledon	United States	Davis Cup
W. Renshaw (G. B.) and E. Renshaw ..	80, 81, 84, 85, 86, 88, 89		Not initiated until 1900
Richard D. Sears (U. S.) and James Dwight		82, 83, 84, 86, 87	
Richard D. Sears (U. S.) and Joseph Clark		85	
Holcombe Ward and George P. Sheldon, Jr. (U. S.)		97, 98	
Holcombe Ward and Dwight F. Davis	01	99, 00, 01	00
Holcombe Ward and Beals C. Wright		04, 05, 06	
Reginald F. Doherty and Hugh L. Doherty (G. B.)	97, 98, 99, 00, 01, 03, 05	02, 03	02, 03, 04, 05, 06
Harold H. Hackett and Fred B. Alexander (U. S.)	07, 08, 09, 10		
Harold H. Hackett and Maurice E. McLoughlin			13
Norman E. Brookes and Anthony F. Wilding (A)	07, 14		08, 09, 14
Norman E. Brookes and Alfred W. Dunlop			11, 12
Norman E. Brookes and Gerald L. Patterson		19	19
Anthony F. Wilding and Norman E. Brookes (A)	07, 14		08, 09, 14
Anthony F. Wilding and M. J. G. Ritchie	08, 10		
William T. Tilden, 2nd, and Vincent Richards (U. S.)		18, 21, 22	
William T. Tilden, 2nd, and B. I. C. Norton		23	
William T. Tilden, 2nd, and Francis T. Hunter	27	27	27
William T. Tilden, 2nd, and William M. Johnston			20, 24
William T. Tilden, 2nd, and R. Norris Williams			23
Vincent Richards and William T. Tilden, 2nd (U. S.)		18, 21, 22	
Vincent Richards and R. Norris Williams		25, 26	25, 26
Vincent Richards and Francis T. Hunter	24		
Jacques Brugnon and Jean Borotra (F)	32, 33		33
Jacques Brugnon and Henri Cochet	26, 28		30, 31
Jean Borotra and Jacques Brugnon (F)a	32, 33		33
Jean Borotra and Rene Lacoste	25		
Jean Borotra and Henri Cochet			28
George M. Lott, Jr. and John F. Hennessey (U. S.)		28	
George M. Lott, Jr. and John H. Doeg		29, 30	
George M. Lott, Jr. and John Van Ryn	31		
George M. Lott, Jr. and Lester R. Stoefen	34	33, 34	34
John Van Ryn and Wilmer L. Allison (U. S.)	29, 30	31, 35	29, 32
John Van Ryn and George M. Lott, Jr.	31		
Wilmer L. Allison and John Van Ryn (U. S.)	29, 30	31, 35	29, 32

TABLE II (*Continued*)

	TOURNAMENT AND YEAR OF VICTORY		
Name and Nationality	Wimbledon	*United States*	*Davis Cup*
Adrian K. Quist and John H. Crawford (A)	35		36
Adrian K. Quist and John E. Bromwich[b]	50	39	38, 39
J. Donald Budge and C. Gene Mako (U. S.)	37, 38	36, 38	37
John E. Bromwich and Adrian K. Quist (A)[b]	50	39	38, 39
John E. Bromwich and Colin Long			47
John E. Bromwich and William Sidwell		49	49
John E. Bromwich and Frank Sedgman	48	50	50
John A. Kramer and Frederick R. Schroeder, Jr. (U. S.)		40, 41	46
John A. Kramer and Frank A. Parker		43	
John A. Kramer and Tom Brown	46		
John A. Kramer and Robert Falkenberg	47		
Gardnar Mulloy and William F. Talbert (U. S.)		42, 45, 46, 48	48
Gardnar Mulloy and Budge Patty	57		
Frank Sedgman and John E. Bromwich (A)	48	50	50
Frank Sedgman and Kenneth MacGregor (A)	51, 52	51	51, 52
Lewis Hoad and Kenneth Rosewall (A)	53, 56	56	56
Lewis Hoad and Rex Hartwig	55		55
Neale A. Fraser and Ashley J. Cooper (A)		57	
Neale A. Fraser and Roy Emerson	59, 61	59, 60	59, 60, 61
Roy Emerson and Neale A. Fraser (A)	59, 61	59, 60	59, 60, 61
Roy Emerson and Rodney Laver			62
Roy Emerson and Fred Stolle		65, 66	
R. Dennis Ralston (U. S.) and Rafael Osuna	60		
R. Dennis Ralston and Charles McKinley		61, 63, 64	63, 64

A = Australia

G. B. = Great Britain

F = France

U. S. = United States

[a] Borotra and Brugnon together or with various partners shared the French Doubles Championship ten times between 1922 and 1936.

[b] Bromwich and Quist won the Australian Doubles Championship eight consecutive times, 1938 to 1951.

that the two world wars terminated the careers of such stars as Tony Wilding and Joe Hunt, and interrupted probable long winning streaks for other outstanding players.

The experts agree that of these famous players perhaps the best were Holcombe Ward, Hugh L. (Little Do) Doherty, George M. Lott, Jr., and John E. Bromwich. These players share two important characteristics: each was the steady member and play-maker of his team; and each was a team player capable of joining with almost any partner to form a winning combination. The best teams in doubles history were formed when these men, whose finesse maneuvered the opposition into

TABLE III

Name and Nationality	Tournament and Year of Victory	
	Wimbledon	United States
Mrs. H. H. Wightman and Edith E. Rotch (U. S.)		09, 10
Mrs. H. H. Wightman and Eleanora Sears		11, 15
Mrs. H. H. Wightman and Helen N. Wills	24	24, 28
Elizabeth Ryan and Eleanor Goss (U. S.)		26
Elizabeth Ryan and A. M. Morton	14	
Elizabeth Ryan and Mlle S. Lenglen	19, 20, 21, 22, 23, 25	
Elizabeth Ryan and Helen N. Wills	27, 30	
Elizabeth Ryan and Mme S. Methieu	33, 34	
Elizabeth Ryan and Mary K. Browne	26	
Helen N. Wills and Mrs. M. Z. Jessup (U. S.)		22
Helen N. Wills and Mrs. H. H. Wightman		24, 28
Helen N. Wills and Mary K. Browne		25
Helen N. Wills and Elizabeth Ryan	27, 30	
Sarah Palfrey and Betty Nuthall (U. S.)		30
Sarah Palfrey and Helen Jacobs		32, 34, 35
Sarah Palfrey and Alice Marble	38, 39	37, 38, 39, 40
Sarah Palfrey and Margaret E. Osborne		41
Margaret Osborne Dupont and Sarah Palfrey (U. S.)		41
Margaret Osborne Dupont and A. Louise Brough	46, 48, 49, 50, 54	42, 43, 44, 45, 46, 47, 48, 49, 50, 55, 56, 57
A. Louise Brough and Margaret Osborne Dupont (U. S.)	46, 48, 49, 50, 54	42, 43, 44, 45, 46, 47, 48, 49, 50, 55, 56, 57
Shirley Fry and Doris Hart (U. S.)	51, 52, 53	51, 52, 53, 54
Darlene R. Hard and Althea Gibson (U. S.)	57	
Darlene R. Hard and Jeanne Arth	59	58, 59
Darlene R. Hard and Maria E. Bueno	60, 63	60, 62
Darlene R. Hard and Lesley Turner		61
Maria E. Bueno (Brazil) and Althea Gibson	58	
Maria E. Bueno and Darlene R. Hard	60, 63	60, 62
Maria E. Bueno and Billie J. Moffitt	65	
Maria E. Bueno and Nancy Richey	66	66
Mrs. Billie Jean M. King (U. S.) and Mrs. Karen H. Susman	61, 62	64
Mrs. Billie Jean M. King and Maria E. Bueno	65	
Mrs. Billie Jean M. King and Rosemary Casals	67	67

weak returns, teamed with a smashing partner who could put away the weak returns in a decisive manner. Some of the more famous smashing types of player were Beals Wright, R. F. Doherty, John Doeg, Lester Stoefen, Ellsworth Vines, Don Budge, and Jack Kramer.

Another factor important in the success of these famous doubles combinations was teamwork. To a large degree it was teamwork that enabled such teams as the Doherty brothers, Ward and Wright, Hackett and Alexander, Brugnon and Borotra, Bromwich and Quist, and Allison and Van Ryn to write doubles history. Perhaps the most striking example of pure teamwork and determination was the Kinsey brothers, who won the United States championship in 1924 largely on team play rather than fundamental tennis superiority.

The dream team of all times (mentioned in Chapter I) would probably have been produced if George Lott or John Bromwich and Don Budge or Jack Kramer could have played together. Between them they would have represented a combination of the tops in doubles craft on the one hand and all-out hitting power on the other. If they could have added to their game the superb teamwork of the Doherty brothers or Allison and Van Ryn, they would have been unbeatable.

A potentially phenomenal team was the "whiz kids" combine from Australia, Lewis Hoad and Ken Rosewall, who won the Wimbledon, Australian, and French doubles championships when just eighteen years old. A shift to the professional ranks cut short their chances at a long string of amateur titles.

The next great doubles players to come along were the fine all-around Australian, Roy Emerson, and the talented American shot maker, Dennis Ralston. Between them, playing with various partners, they dominated the doubles tournaments of the world for eight years.

Many of the best singles players, men like Big Bill Tilden, the greatest of all time, Little Bill Johnston, William Larned, Maurice Mc-Loughlin, Fred Perry, Rene Lacoste, Malcolm Whitman, Bunny Austin, Ellsworth Vines, Bitsy Grant, and Sidney Wood, were not outstanding as doubles players. Despite Tilden's brilliance off the ground, even he rated himself poor at doubles. Considering the large number of fine individual players the world of tennis has seen, it is remarkable how few really great doubles teams have been developed. This is due largely to the great complexity of doubles. Also, it is due in part to the greater popularity and prestige the singles championship has enjoyed in the past—a popularity that has tended to retard the development of the art and science of doubles.

Among the women Bunny Ryan stands out as a heady player. Over a period of twenty years she won major tournaments as the steady play-maker with a variety of partners. Another perennial champion was little Sarah Palfrey. Deserving special mention is Mrs. Hazel Wightman, grand lady of the Longwood Cricket Club, a national champion some forty-five times and a developer of many champions. Perhaps the best ladies' team developed to date is the championship combination of Louise Brough and Margaret Osborne Dupont. They played a forcing game, resembling that of the men, which won them twelve U. S. and 5 Wimbledon titles! Another ladies' doubles star is the graceful Brazilian, Maria Bueno. She has all the shots and her smooth, seemingly effortless execution makes the game look ridiculously easy. The most recent U. S. additions to the list, Darlene Hard and Billie Jean Moffitt King, both copy effectively the aggressive serve and volley game of the men.

What happens when you mix the sexes? Most top male stars refuse to be quoted on what they think about the game of mixed doubles. But rather than stir up trouble with the ladies, let us testify to their importance: mixed doubles matches depend *almost entirely* on the skill of the female members. Over a twenty-year period, nineteen out of twenty Mixed Doubles Championships were won by teams having lady members who were, in that same year, U. S. Women's Doubles champions. Almost any male player could manage to win with a top girl to carry him, as shown by the fact that only nine of the twenty male winners were also Men's Doubles champions. This may not prove which is the stronger sex, but it gives the girls a strong talking point.

One of the uses of history, the old adage tells us, is to show how little is new under the sun. A study of tennis history leaves the same impression. Most of the suggestions for the tactics of modern doubles were made years ago. However, it was not until recently that they have been put into effect with devastating force.

During the first U. S. Doubles Championship at Newport in 1881, all but three teams entered played with all four players standing back of the base line. The winners, C. M. Clark and F. W. Taylor, and one other team used the system of one up and one back—that is, with the server's partner playing the net position. One team, Richard D. Sears and Dr. James Dwight, which later won the title several times, experimented with both players along the service court line after serving.

In 1883 the Clark brothers went to England to play the famous Renshaw brothers. They took a trouncing and thereupon adopted the British style of play, which dictated that the partners must remain parallel. Both played on the base line or both moved in to the net position together. The distance they played from the net was determined by the depth from which the opponents were striking the ball. The one-up one-back system was thus found to be untenable at this early date, although one can still see it in use by club players now, over sixty years later!

In 1888 Oliver S. Campbell and Valentine G. Hall, who won the U. S. title, practiced the art of following service in to the net. In commenting on the innovation later, Campbell wrote: "It became very apparent in this tournament that a doubles team that continually stayed at net, both on their own service and as often as possible on their opponent's, were at a decided advantage; and all our doubles championship teams, from that date up to the present time, have adopted this style of play." It is interesting to note that the Australians adopted these tactics quite independently just two years later, in 1890.

In the early 1890's the Americans turned the tables on visiting British doubles players. The error in British tactics, of which they took advantage, was a tendency to volley from a deep position near the service line. This made low shots down the middle or at wide angles difficult to handle and forced the British to volley up, thus taking the sting out of their shots.

As early as 1893 Dr. Dwight uttered this astute prediction of the modern game of doubles: "The theoretical game is for all four players to be forward at once and all volleying. The game resolves itself into a question of which side will miss or lose its position first." If more players had read and understood the wisdom of these words, it would not have taken so long to develop the game of today. The sad fact is that some of our current players still have not learned the lesson well enough.

About 1899 the American players Ward, Davis, and Wright tried out a new formation for the serving team. This was a defense against a strong cross-court return of service, and it placed the server's partner at the net position on the same side of the court as the server. It permitted the net man to get properly positioned for the cross-court return, while the server moved in diagonally to the net position to cover a down-the-line return. Interestingly, this reverse formation was also experimented with at almost exactly the same time by an Australian named Kidston. Since the Australians have exploited the formation more in international play than the Americans, it has been dubbed the "Australian formation" by sports writers.

At the turn of the century came the inauguration of the Davis Cup matches. These famous contests brought together the world's top players, and this caused a rapid development of the game of doubles. The great Doherty brothers rose to fame in this era and succeeded in carrying off fifteen major titles (see Table II). The international matches between the Americans Ward, Davis, and Wright and the Dohertys served to start doubles on the road to popularity. The sportsmanship of the brothers always won for them the hearts of the gallery.

The Dohertys did much for the technical advance of doubles. Their team play was near perfection: each knew the other's game thoroughly, could thus anticipate his partner's shot and move unerringly to the proper position for the next return. In addition, they gave a lot of thought to the game and experimented with court position and tactics. During their first visits to the United States they tended to volley from too deep a position, as had the earlier British invaders. However, experience in this country, coupled with the suggestion of Wilfred Baddeley, one of the early British doubles authorities, led the Dohertys to adopt the closer volleying position. They showed a much better return of service than the Americans—a low, fast return, rather than the lob that was in vogue here. Perhaps the most valuable contribution the brothers made was the concept of a new defense for the receiving team. At this stage in doubles history the serving team, which took the net, had such an advantage over the receiving team, which usually hung back of the base line, that some experts were recommending increasing the width of the doubles court or abolishing the second service to make matters more even. The Dohertys introduced a defense formation that placed the partner of the receiver at a modified net position, permitting him to take the offensive by volleying any poor return from the server as he moved in to the net. Mention is made in 1903 of their initial struggles with this formation—struggles that were not too successful against the fast serves of the Americans. Early tennis writers held that the formation was unsound and should be abandoned. However, the Dohertys kept trying it, and pictures taken in 1906 show them employing it against the superb Australians, Brookes and Wilding.

The wily Australians lost no time in recognizing how it improved the chances of the receiving team to break service. They adopted this defense formation, as did all the great doubles teams which have since been turned out by the Aussies. In fact, the Australians have used it so widely that they are erroneously considered by many to have invented the formation. However, no less an authority than the great Australian, Tony Wilding, wrote a book published before his death in World War I, crediting the Dohertys with teaching him the partner-of-the-receiver-at-net idea.

The Americans also contributed to the development of doubles at the turn of the century. Perhaps their most significant contribution was made by Holcombe Ward. After observing the effects of spin on a tennis ball Ward practiced a new type of service, which he finally perfected in 1897. The ball was thrown farther back and farther to the left, so that the racquet moved from left to right across the ball, thus imparting considerable spin. The ball took a high, curving flight, then bounded high to the backhand of the receiver. Ward found that the serve gave him more time to get to the net, was easy to control, and was difficult for the receiver to deal with effectively. It was christened the American twist service, and was enthusiastically received everywhere. It has since become the standard delivery of doubles players all over the world.

Ward, together with his partner, Beals Wright, also helped to improve the position of the receiver. They practiced standing inside the base line, taking the serve on the rise and hitting the ball down at the server's feet as he came in. This tactic has also been universally adopted.

Every good offense usually produces a good defense, and the American twist service was no exception. Besides taking the ball on the rise, Beals Wright worked on the development of a counterattacking return. This stroke has since become known as the dink shot. It is a soft, angled chop or slice shot, hit so as to clear the net by a slim margin and drop precipitously. Its purpose was to embarrass the server, who has been able to get well in toward the net behind his twist serve. The dink shot forces him to dig the ball out of the ground and volley it up into the air from below the level of the net, thus giving the receiving team a good opportunity of winning the point. The dink was further improved by such players as Lott and Bromwich, who drove opposing servers wild trying to volley the delicate shots effectively.

Going one step further, the Australians have dreamed up a devilish maneuver which we have christened "the drift." The drift is aimed at taking advantage of a well-stroked dink or other cross-court return of service. It is carried out by the partner of the receiver, who is stationed in the modified net position of the Doherty brothers. If he notes that the receiver is making an effective return of service, which will in most cases cause the server to volley up and cross-court, the net man deserts his position and moves across the court and closer to the net. That is, he makes a semi-poach on the side of his partner and is in position either to put away any weak volley by the server or to force the server to volley wide, where the chances for error are considerably greater. Messrs. Sedgman, Rose, and Hoad are particularly clever at this drifting tactic, and some Americans such as Schroeder have also picked up the idea effectively.

Another tactic developed by the Australians is "packing the center." Whenever the two partners are at net, they position themselves so they are closer to each other than to either of the outside alley lines. This position turns the court-covering percentages in their favor, for most volleys are made toward the center of the court, where the net is lower and the chances of hitting the ball out are less. It is fascinating to note that this strategy had been used years ago by the American teams of Ward and Wright, and later Allison and Van Ryn, but once again it took the ever-alert Aussies to realize its value and bring it to maximum effectiveness.

Packing the center has had much to do with Australian victories in thirteen out of fifteen of the top doubles matches over the past five years. But a possible counterstrategy is appearing. In the finals of the 1954 U. S. National Doubles Championship, Seixas and Trabert defeated Hoad and Rosewall by volleying down the line or angling from the center toward the open territory beyond. To counteract the counter, however, the Aussies are now moving a little closer to the net.

It is not known who first started using signals for poaching. However, the system used during 1954 by Seixas and Trabert has brought signaling one stage closer to perfection. Before the server makes his delivery, the net man turns and faces the base line so that the opponents cannot see the signal. The signal is passed on any serve, first or second, at the election of the net man. The mere fact that he turns to give a signal tends to upset the receiver, breaking his concentration, often causing him to take his eye off the ball and hit a poor return. The victories of Seixas and Trabert in the 1953 and 1954 Davis Cup Challenge Rounds and the 1954 U. S. Doubles Championship are attributed largely to the worrisome effect of excellent poaching against Hartwig, Hoad, and Rosewall. The best defense against the presignaled poach is to mix up the normal cross-court return of service with a number of drives hit down the line—low enough so that they cannot be volleyed offensively.

The many offensive and defensive tactics, and court position and types of strokes required to carry them off, will be discussed and explained in greater detail in the chapters which follow. This fascinating duel between new offenses and new offsetting defenses will continue to go on as long as the great game of doubles is played.

CHAPTER III

The Game

At this point let us undertake an over-all examination of the game of doubles, thus to provide a solid framework for the finer points and tactics of the game.

Of the general features of topflight doubles play, four outweigh the rest:

1. *Offense.*

To win at doubles the offense must be obtained and maintained. The offensive position in doubles is at the net. Both members of the team must concentrate on getting to the net and remaining there on every point.

2. *Teamwork.*

Doubles is a team game. Team play begins with respect for and congeniality with one's partner. Hours of practicing together, learning one another's tennis games, planning strategy and tactics, establishing optimum court positions for varying situations, studying the weaknesses in the games of the opposition, encouraging and steadying one's partner during play—all these and more are essential to superior doubles teamwork. Individual brilliance must be submerged and coordinated team effort emphasized.

3. *Anticipation.*

Play is so much faster in doubles than in singles, particularly when both teams are volleying at each other at point-blank range, that anticipating the nature and direction of the opponents' shots becomes absolutely essential. The "impossible" returns, whether they are made in championship or week-end doubles, are the results of practiced, split-second anticipation. And anticipation can be developed only by a careful study of the position of the ball with respect to the player; the opponent's tennis personality; the position of his wrist, arm, and feet during different types of shots; his habits under certain conditions; and give-away glances in the direction of his aim point.

4. *Concentration.*

The tactical generalship, teamwork, and speed of good doubles require constant concentration. To outmaneuver the opponents requires outthinking them. A poor shot or a strategic blunder may be rectified in singles play, but usually means sudden death in doubles. Remember that any relaxation of concentration results in letting down one's partner. Creative planning during the progress of the match should permit a team to put sufficient variety into its game to keep the opponents off balance.

In 1948 Tilden wrote: "In all the years I have been on the courts I have seen very few people with what I call the scientific approach to tennis." He went on to say that "the scientific approach" includes a knowledge of the mechanics of stroke production, the psychology of pressure properly applied, and the search for new methods to improve the game.

Tilden hit the nail on the head: to analyze the game of doubles properly demands more—much more—than a perfunctory look. In pursuit of the scientific approach, the authors have collected detailed data on a number of championship matches over the past seven years at the National Doubles Championship at Longwood, at the Newport Casino Tournament, and at professional matches. Data were gathered on the total number of various strokes, the types of strokes which resulted in winning points for entire matches, position play, and tactics used in forcing openings to permit winning placements and so on. These data, recorded here in several tables, are most revealing. The tables will be referred to in a general way in this chapter, and in more detail later on.

Let us look first at the total shots made in the two matches summarized in Table IV.

Table IV makes at least three outstanding points. First, it shows strikingly that the percentile frequency of stroke types varies but little from match to match. Second, it reveals that the most frequently used stroke types in doubles are at the net, volley, and overhead. Next in line are the first service and the return of service. Together they constitute almost four fifths of the shots made. Third, it shows clearly that the ground stroke, so important in singles, is relegated to the background in doubles. The only ground stroke prominent in doubles is the vital return of service, which, by the rules, must be played as a ground stroke. (Incidentally, there are more overheads than lobs recorded in Table IV because ground strokes that happened to sail high enough to be hit with an overhead were recorded as ground strokes rather than lobs.)

TABLE IV

NUMBER AND PERCENTILE FREQUENCY OF STROKE TYPES DURING COMPLETE DOUBLES MATCHES (OMITTING ERRORS)

Match 1 (both teams; 604 total strokes)

	First Service	Second Service	Ground Strokes Return of Service	Other	Volley	Overhead	Lob
Number ...	140	43	129	51	145	56	40
Per cent ...	23	7	21	9	24	9	7

Match 2—Team A (Winner; 382 total strokes)

	First Service	Second Service	Return of Service	Other	Volley	Overhead	Lob
Number ...	84	17	105	36	113	16	11
Per cent ...	22	4	27	10	30	4	3

Match 2—Team B (Loser; 405 total strokes)

	First Service	Second Service	Return of Service	Other	Volley	Overhead	Lob
Number ...	96	27	81	53	111	17	20
Per cent ...	24	7	20	13	27	4	5

More important than the number of the various strokes is the type of stroke used in winning the points in doubles. Data taken on four championship matches during 1949 and 1950, and several club matches during 1955, are recorded in Table V.

TABLE V

SUMMARY OF NUMBER AND PERCENTILE FREQUENCY OF POINT-WINNING STROKE TYPES

165 Games Championship Doubles Play

	First Serve	Second Serve	Ground Strokes Return of Service	Other	Volley	Overhead	Lob	Total Winners
No. Winners .	184	14	116	125	409	136	25	1,009
Per cent	18	1	12	12	41	14	2	

85 Games Club Doubles Play

	First Serve	Second Serve	Return of Service	Other	Volley	Overhead	Lob	Total Winners
No. Winners .	87	22	86	94	133	70	22	514
Per cent	17	4	17	18	26	14	4	

The most striking feature of Table V is the importance of net play: 55 per cent of all winners were made at the net position. Note, too, how many more winners were produced by the first service than by second service. This is due largely to errors on the return of first service rather than aces (as shown later in Table VIII and Chapters IV and V). The negligible importance of the lob as an outright point winner is a tribute to the effectiveness of the smashing overhead play of today, as well as to the retrieving ability obtained through anticipation.

Week-enders should study the difference between the championship and club portions of Table V. No question about it, the experts have comparatively better volleys and overheads. They win 55 per cent of points at the net as against 40 per cent by the club players. And the club players lose more points to the ground strokes, return of service, and others. This means they erred on volleys the experts would have made. Therefore, the obvious advice to all doubles players is to practice those volleys—make them good and make them forceful.

A combination of Tables IV and V indicates that approximately five strokes are made during each point, and that the average length of a game is about six points. These tables also evaluate the relative probability of producing a winner by a given stroke (shown in descending comparative values in Table VI). All the probabilities are based on a comparison with the least potent winner, the second service.

TABLE VI

RELATIVE PROBABILITY OF WINNING A POINT WITH A GIVEN TYPE OF STROKE
CONSIDERING THE FREQUENCY OF THE STROKE UTILIZED

	Potency Factor
Overhead	14.5
Volley	9.5
Ground strokes (other than return of service)	7.5
First serve	5
Return of service	3
Lob	2.5
Second service	1 (basis of comparison)

Table VI further emphasizes the importance of the attacking position at the net, where the two most potent shots are the overhead and the volley. And the relative impotency of the return of service is something to think about.

A more complete set of data was taken on a match between Gonzales and Parker, 1949 Wimbledon Doubles Champions, and Bromwich and Sidwell, 1949 United States Doubles Champions. Data from this match, won by the Bromwich team 13-11, 10-8, 10-8, are recorded in Table VII.

Table VII is an excellent capsule exposition of the game of modern doubles. The Australians, under the generalship of John Bromwich, the best amateur doubles player of his time, performed masterfully. Study of the table shows that the Australians won by maintaining control of the net. The total points were 174 for Bromwich and Sidwell as against 150 for Parker and Gonzales. Of this difference of twenty-four points, almost all was produced by volleying, where the Australians led eighty-six winners to sixty-five. In all other stroke departments the two teams had an almost identical number of winners.

Most of the comments on this important table will be reserved for later chapters. However, it is never too early to introduce "lethality"—the percentage of placements obtained by the stroke types used in winning points. With two men to cover a court not much larger than a singles court, placements are difficult to make, and it is vital to know by which strokes they are achieved. Once again the two teams were almost identical in all strokes except volleying, where Bromwich and Sidwell had a total of thirty-five placements as against twenty-six for Gonzales and Parker.

A second complete match was monitored for winners and placements, the better to judge the lethality of stroke types. This time the great Australian teams of Sedgman and McGregor and Hoad and Rosewall were studied (as shown in Table VII A). In this match the two teams were equally effective in net play, but the bigger and more powerful Sedgman-McGregor combine was far more effective in the service department. They won thirty-six points on service as against twenty for Hoad and Rosewall, and twenty-two points on return of service as against eleven.

Table VIII shows once again the strength of the net position in doubles, this time from the standpoint of putting the ball away. Two hundred thirty-one out of two hundred eighty-one placements recorded, or 82 per cent, were made with volleys and overheads. Of all the strokes, the angled overhead and angled volley hit toward the open country beyond the sidelines were the most lethal. Obviously, the expert doubles player must be able to take advantage of openings and weak returns to angle off sure winners. Just as obviously, the overhead hit deep is also high in percentage of placements obtained. These shots are usually hit with terrific speed unless the lob is an excellent one. However, the lethality of the down-the-line and angled ground strokes will surprise many. When the opponents make a relatively weak volley

TABLE VII
STROKES USED IN WINNING POINTS
Total Winners

| | Service | | Return of Service | | Ground Stroke | | | Volley | | | Overhead | | |
	First	Second	Ground Stroke	Lob	Down Line	Angle	Middle	Deep	Angle	Lob	Deep	Angle	Lob
Bromwich-Sidwell													
First set	11	1	5	0	1	2	2	26	11	0	10	2	2
Second set	7	0	4	0	1	1	4	20	4	0	4	0	0
Third set	10	0	4	0	1	1	5	19	6	0	8	1	1
TOTALS	28	1	13	0	3	4	11	65	21	0	22	3	3
Gonzales-Parker													
First set	14	1	3	2	1	2	5	19	5	3	6	2	2
Second set	8	0	5	0	0	1	1	13	6	0	4	2	0
Third set	5	1	4	0	1	0	3	14	5	0	9	2	1
TOTALS	27	2	11	2	2	3	9	46	16	3	19	6	3

Winners by Placements

| | Service | | Return of Service | | Ground Stroke | | | Volley | | | Overhead | | |
	First	Second	Ground Stroke	Lob	Down Line	Angle	Middle	Deep	Angle	Lob	Deep	Angle	Lob
Bromwich-Sidwell													
First set	1	0	0	0	0	1	0	7	4	0	4	2	0
Second set	0	0	0	0	0	0	0	8	2	0	3	0	0
Third set	0	0	1	0	0	0	1	8	6	0	7	1	0
TOTALS	1	0	1	0	0	1	1	23	12	0	14	3	0
Gonzales-Parker													
First set	0	0	0	0	0	0	0	5	3	1	2	1	0
Second set	1	0	0	0	0	1	0	4	6	0	4	2	0
Third set	1	0	0	0	1	0	0	5	2	0	6	2	0
TOTALS	2	0	0	0	1	1	0	14	11	1	12	5	0

TABLE VII-A
Strokes Used in Winning Points

Total Winners

	Service		Return of Service			Ground Stroke				Volley		Overhead		
	First	Second	Drive	Dink	Lob	Down Line	Middle	Angle	Deep	Angle	Lob	Deep	Angle	Lob
Sedgman-McGregor	32	4	15	7	0	4	2	1	29	8	0	5	2	1
Hoad-Rosewall	19	1	8	3	0	1	6	0	29	6	0	6	7	1

Winners by Placements

	Service		Return of Service			Ground Stroke				Volley		Overhead		
	First	Second	Drive	Dink	Lob	Down Line	Middle	Angle	Deep	Angle	Lob	Deep	Angle	Lob
Sedgman-McGregor	0	0	2	1	0	2	0	0	10	4	0	4	2	0
Hoad-Rosewall	0	0	2	0	0	0	1	0	8	4	0	2	6	0

Semi-Final Match U. S. National Championship 1952; Won by Sedgman-McGregor 5-7, 6-2, 6-4, 6-2

TABLE VIII
Analysis of Winners and Placements
Data Collected from Four Complete Championship Matches

	First Serve	Second Serve	Return of Service	Ground Strokes				Volleys		Overhead		
				Down Line	Angle	Down Middle	Deep	Angle	Lob	Deep	Angle	Lob
Number of winners	184	14	116	39	25	61	316	93	9	110	46	25
Per cent of winners	18	1	11	4	3	6	30	9	1	11	4	2
Number of placements	7	0	7	18	9	9	83	57	1	49	41	0
Lethality (per cent of winners in each type of stroke resulting in placements)	4	0	6	46	36	15	26	60	11	45	89	0

to the sidelines at the mid-court area, they open up a wide angle of possible return. Thus the premium on control of ground strokes, which permits one to punch a placement through the opening down the line or cross-court. The deep volleys, which represent by far the greatest per cent of winners, are not so high on lethality. They are more likely to force errors than to win placements, since the area open for outright winners is limited. The remaining strokes produce so few placements that for now they can almost be discounted. (The anticipation and court-covering abilities of the topflight tennis tandems are quite remarkable.)

Consider for a moment the sad but inevitable subject of errors. Even in championship doubles play there are about 2.2 errors made for every placement gained. The figure is startling and eloquent. It proves as nothing else can the old doubles truism: keep the ball in play no matter how hard you have to scramble—the opponents will often oblige by hitting the ball out or in the net. Of the errors made in doubles, nets lead outs on a three-to-two ratio. (In singles the two are about equal.) The explanation is simple: The players keep the ball low and risk netting rather than give the opposing net man an easy forcing volley. One monitored match showed that in a red-hot set Bromwich and Sedgman scored two placements for every error—but this is indeed a rarity.

In selecting a long-term partner for doubles, you must find a person you like and respect. The most famous teams in history were generally made of players who became fast friends both on and off the court. Most experts agree that teamwork is approximately 25 per cent of the game. And teamwork can be achieved only by years of practice. Cochet estimates that the molding of a team takes five to six years of playing and practicing together. Out of such experience evolves teamwork that is beautiful to watch. The players move as if coordinated by a single brain, each knowing what his partner will do under any given condition. An example of splendid teamwork is shown in Figure 2. It is the diagram of a well-remembered point played by Allison and Van Ryn against Hines and Culley in the Eastern Grass Court Championship at Rye in 1936. Winning under the circumstances shown in Figure 2 means more than just taking a point; it boosts the morale of the saving team and dampens the spirits of the apparent winners, who have already counted the point, then see it slip away.

Again, in selecting a partner try to find one with a complementary game. Experience has shown that many of the best combinations have a steady player who sets up the plays and a power player who can put

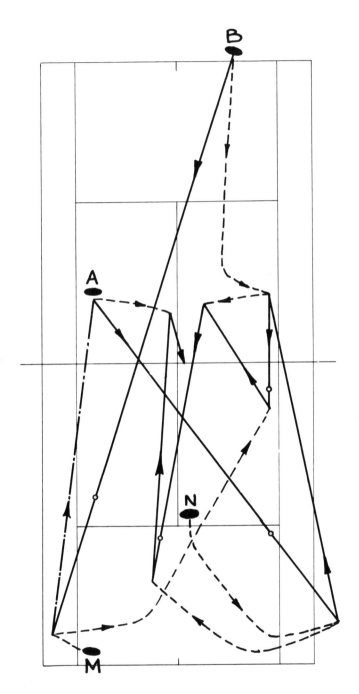

Figure 2

Hines, server **B,** hit a hard service to the backhand of receiver **M,** Allison, who returned a weak lob. Culley, net man **A,** smashed the lob at a wicked angle cross-court for an apparent winner. However, Van Ryn, **N,** anticipated, got his racquet on the ball, and returned a forehand down the line. This left the whole right side of the court open; Hines, who had followed his serve in, moved to his left in anticipation and was waiting at the net for the return to hit a short drop volley. Once again this looked like a certain winner. However, Allison, anticipating Hines' shot, had noted Van Ryn would not be able to get back into position. So he got set for it and made a well-concealed fast break to cover the shot after Hines had committed himself. He retrieved the drop shot and hit a topped drive toward the middle. Hines moved over and volleyed the ball to the left side of the court, which Allison had just deserted. For the third time it looked as though the point had been won; but Van Ryn came back fast, crossed over to cover the opening in Allison's court, and drove a backhand down the middle which Culley netted. Thus, Allison and Van Ryn saved a point that looked lost three times.

the ball away. It is best to have a player with a strong cross-court forehand return of service and backhand volley to play the right side, and a player with a strong backhand and a good forehand volley should play the left side. The left-court player must have a strong overhead; he will be called on to take the majority of lobs, since those down the middle are on his forehand. Most experts think that if one of the players is left-handed he should consider playing the right side in order to put both forehands in the center. However, several famous left-handers—for example, Norman Brookes, Beals Wright, and Mervyn Rose—have played the left-hand side. All things being equal, the stronger player should play the backhand side, as the deciding points are played in this court. Once the partners have chosen sides, each should play his own side exclusively, in order to develop smooth teamwork.

But there is more to teamwork than technical proficiency for two. Even the best players have bad streaks, so when your partner is in the doldrums keep calm and offer him encouragement until he has regained his touch. Don't criticize unless you can be constructive. The abilities and tactics of the opponents must be diagnosed in order to take advantage of their weaknesses; so make a plan and hold to it as long as it is successful. Review the situation as the match progresses. Study your mistakes, try to determine why you are making them and how you can avoid repeating them. Be prepared to change tactics at a moment's notice, for while an opponent may have a bad time at the start of a match, continued pounding of his side of the court will boomerang as he begins to find himself in the later stages. Concentrate. Continued concentration on outmaneuvering the opponents may lead to a break in their morale. Think fast and decisively, follow the ball on every play, and don't let up.

A good doubles player reacts instinctively—and loud. The partner best able to judge the flight of the ball yells, "Out," or "Good," or "Bounce it," on doubtful shots. Often such calls have to be made so fast that many players simply shout, "No," on balls that should be allowed to go by, and ignore any calls of "good" except on lobs falling near the lines. When a player anticipates a drop shot ahead of his partner, or when he starts for the net unexpectedly and wants his partner to move in, he should say, "Up." If he hits a weak lob and wants to warn his partner to move toward the base line or to the side to help defend the overhead, he should so indicate with "back" or "over." The players should yell, "Yours," or, "Mine," as the case may be, on shots that either might take. Of course, general teamwork and prearranged tactics on certain shots will obviate the necessity of excessive yelling. And a more deliberate set of signals should be worked out for poaching by the net man on effective serves.

More will be said about teamwork from time to time. Tilden has called doubles a game of position. Coordinated court coverage on offense and defense is essential to topflight play. There can be no lagging in getting into proper position or covering up for your partner if he is drawn out of position. Anticipation means moving to the right place at the right time.

It should be abundantly clear by this time that this game of doubles is complicated. There is no game like it for the continuous pressure of tactical concentration plus split-second timing. The more one studies it, the greater respect it commands.

CHAPTER IV

The Serve

In championship doubles play most sets are won by but a single break-through of service. This makes the loss of service practically unpardonable. In fact, holding service is so vital in doubles that George Lott has been quoted as saying that the serve is the most important shot.

There are some strong arguments to back Lott's opinion. We have already seen in Chapter III that doubles is won by taking and maintaining the offense. The offensive is predicated on control of the net. The successful serve in doubles not only puts the ball in play but also provides a safe journey to the net for the server, putting the serving team in the attacking position at the start of each point. No less a singles authority than Fred Perry agrees that the possession of a strong serve is even more important in doubles than in singles, and it should be remembered (Table IV) that 30 per cent of all strokes made in doubles are serves.

In this chapter the play of the serving team will be taken only as far as preparing for the volley of the return of service. The play from that point on will be discussed in Chapter VI, on Net Play.

The proper normal positions for serving team players A and B, in either the forehand or backhand courts, are shown in Figure 3. The server, B, stands midway between the center of the base line and the sideline, leaving him the shortest route to the proper net position and a better chance (than if he had started from point R) to change direction to meet the return of service. The server's partner, A, stands from six to nine feet from the net and about one foot to the right of center between the line dividing the service courts and the far sideline. More

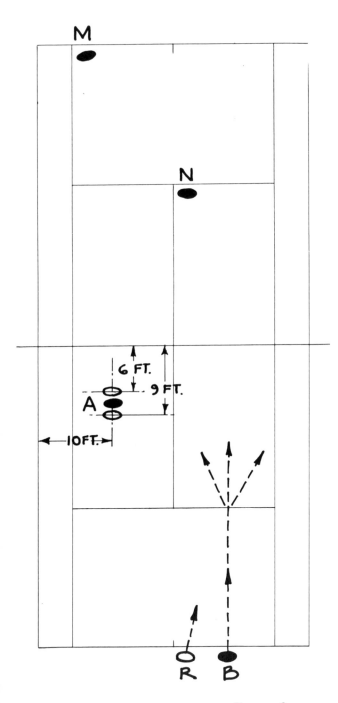

Preferred positions of the net man **A** and the server **B**.

Figure 3

about him later. In addition to these normal positions, there are unconventional positions which the serving team may elect to adopt. These will be dealt with in some detail near the end of this chapter.

The server has two functions. First, he must attempt to force the receiver into making a weak or defensive return of service; and, second, he must follow his service rapidly in to the net to gain the proper position for volleying the return.

To carry out his first function the server commands the weapons of speed, spin, and placement of the service. All outstanding doubles players agree that the most important single objective in serving is to put the *first* service into play. Miss Bunny Ryan and George Lott were particularly insistent on this point. For the receiver, fearing an attempt for an ace, invariably plays further back on the first serve than on the second, thus giving the server valuable additional time to reach the proper net position. As Table IV shows, top teams successfully deliver *80 per cent* of their first services.

The results of merely putting the first serve in play are quite dramatic. Table V, based on data taken at Longwood, shows that 18 per cent of the outright winners result from first serves, whereas only 1 per cent result from second serves. Also, Table VI shows that the first serve ranks fourth in potency among all doubles strokes; while the second service ranks last. This analysis was carried further in a National Doubles semi-final match played by Mulloy and Talbert. They were able to win (either outright or through forcing errors) 80 per cent of the points in which they got their first services into play. However, they were able to win only 48 per cent of the points played from their second services. Striking confirmation was obtained in a professional match that pitted Kramer and Segura against Sedgman and McGregor. These four great servers won 70 per cent of all points they served. However, while the servers won 82 per cent of all points when the first serve was successfully put into play, they were able to win only 24 per cent of points played from their second serves! A final bit of information to nail down the case for the first serve. In the 1953 National Doubles final between Rose and Seixas and Sedgman and McGregor, data taken showed that the net players were able to poach (or move to the center to cut off returns) on good first serves and win fifteen points while losing only four; but they were *never* able to poach successfully on second serve.

The serve in doubles is quite different from that in singles. It must, obviously, be well controlled. In order to force a defensive return, it must also be well placed. Since tennis players, excepting a few notables like Budge and Frankie Parker, are weaker on the backhand side, the serve should generally be to the backhand. It should also be deep in the service court, and it must give the server time to follow in safely to the net position. These demands point to American twist service as the ideal type of delivery for doubles. The twist is easy to control, allows the server (even if a worn-out old man) plenty of time to reach the net position; and the spin imparted to the ball causes a bounce angling high to the backhand—the most difficult of all spots from which to make an offensive return. Consequently, the American twist serve is used as the standard delivery by almost all of topflight doubles players, including most of those players gifted with a "big" serve. For example, consider the data taken on Pancho Gonzales during the 1949 season. In the finals of the National Singles Championship at Forest Hills he served twenty-seven aces against Ted Schroeder during a sixty-seven-game, five-set match; but he succeeded in getting his tremendous first serve in only 59 per cent of the time. By way of contrast, in the quarter-finals and semi-finals of the National Doubles he relied almost entirely on the surer twist service. True, he served just four aces in 103 games, but he *did* put into play about 75 per cent of his first serves. Again, in the Kramer and Segura versus Sedgman and McGregor match, these "big" serve artists slowed down their first serves in order to get 75 per cent of first serves into play.

It may seem surprising that the flat, cannonball serve made famous by such outstanding singles players as McLoughlin, Tilden, Vines, Budge, Kramer, and Gonzales is not recommended for doubles. Although the cannonball will often force a defensive return, it is difficult to control consistently. This lack of control makes for two disadvantages. First, the server wastes a lot of energy hitting faults, all of which he must follow partway in to the net. (In fact, the defending United States doubles champions, Aussies Sedgman and McGregor, were beaten in five sets in the 1952 finals largely because they tired themselves out hitting and following hard serves in the first three of the five sets.) Second, a fault on first service allows the receiver to move in for the second service, giving him a much better chance to take the offensive away from the server. Data show that the receiver will get in to the net six times as often on successful returns of the *second* service as on successful returns of first service.

The cannonball serve has other drawbacks. The faster travel of the ball cuts down the time the server has to get to the net. After slamming a cannonball the server may end up slightly off balance and lose a valuable split-second recovering. In a word, the cannonball is a poor offensive risk in doubles, and when it is returned crisply it means trouble for the serving team.

Yet the average week-end doubles player seems determined to lambaste the ball and to ignore the importance of getting his first serve safely into play. Actually this is no more than an adolescent effort to impress. Against any kind of fair competition he will invariably end up with egg all over his face—throwing away many points and wearing himself in the process. Just remember, even the big serve experts slow their first serve down, and for good reason. So should you!

Most of the best doubles players not only prefer to use the safer twist serve, but they hit it about three-quarters speed in order to exert maximum control and gain more time to reach the net. A slow, well-executed twist lets the server take three priceless steps further in to the net than the cannonball serve. To counter the receiver moving in, the second serve should be paced almost as fast as the first.

In recommending the varied use of twist serve we do not mean, however, that the fast serve or the slice serve should be avoided entirely. The server must have these serves at his command, and should use them from time to time to keep the receiver off balance. An occasional serve to the forehand corner will prevent the receiver from moving over to run around the twist serve. The use of different spin will also tend to upset the receiver and draw poor returns. John Doeg, Don Budge, and Jack Kramer were particularly adept at firing a fast ace at a critical moment when the receiver was a step out of position, or was moving the wrong way, or had let his guard down.

The club player often cannot picture himself being able to deliver the first and second serves at about equal speed. However, the American twist serve is so simple to learn and to control that you will be surprised how quickly you can acquire this skill and lord it over your rivals.

The service is a duel between the server and the receiver, with each trying to gain an advantage so that the second shot by his team can be an offensive one. This means the server must continually study the receiver, his stance, actions, and habits, and try continually to outguess him. The odds favor the server because he begins with the offense. He must play this advantage to the utmost.

Let us consider in detail now the service to the forehand court. The server must first decide where to try to place the serve. The preferred aim point is position 1 (Figure 4). Here's why:

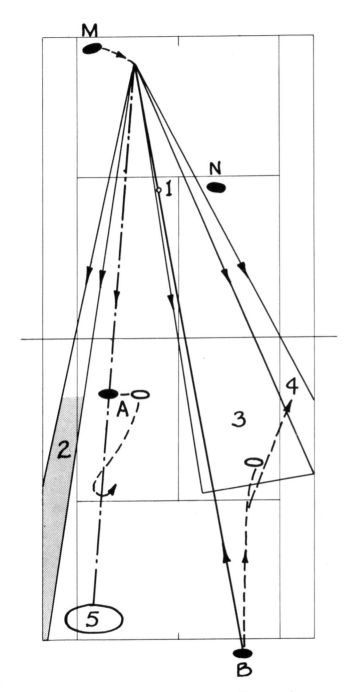

Figure 4

An American twist service placed in area 1 is the best opening gambit for the serving team and gives the server the safest journey to the net.

A return to area 2 is unlikely, since great accuracy is required to hit that narrow angle over the high portion of the net. This permits net man **A** to make the server's job easier. On seeing the serve bounce at area 1 and the receiver commit himself to a cross-court return, net man **A** should slide over to cover the center of the court. Then server **B** can come up wide to cover backhands or run-around forehands hit to area 3, or sharply angled shots hit to area 4. Shots to area 4 must be of the slow dink variety, hit to pass over the higher portion of the net and yet stay in the court, thus giving the server more time to swerve and cover them. Lobs hit by the receiver from the middle to area 5 can be handled effectively by net man **A**, who can drop back and play them on his strong forehand overhead. A serve to area 1 puts the serving team in the best offensive position.

a. It is on the backhand side, which, as has already been noted, is generally the weaker side of the receiver.

b. The angles of return open to the receiver are a minimum.

c. A lob hit from point 1 over the server's partner at net will, in general, go to his strong forehand side, which permits him to deal with it more effectively.

By way of contrast, let us consider what conditions the server must face if he elects to serve wide to point 6. Figure 5 shows the disadvantages involved. In the first place the receiver will be hitting from his more powerful forehand side. Second, the angles of return open to the receiver are much wider: perfect court coverage by the serving team is practically impossible. Finally, a lob hit over the net man can be placed easily on his weaker backhand side by the receiver.

Obviously the server should use point 1 as his aim point in the great majority of cases. The only exceptions should be for purposes of tactical surprise, to keep the opponents off balance. Sometimes surprise is effective on the second serve too. For example, if the server notices that the receiver tends to move in and run around the second serve to slam it with his forehand, he can often catch the receiver off balance by slicing his second serve to the forehand corner. The change will often draw a weak return. Certainly the club player has every reason to hit to the left, as the week-end opponent almost invariably has a weaker backhand than forehand.

The depth, as well as the speed and placement of service, means time to the serving team. The deep, twist service hit about three-fourths speed gives the server time to get well in to the net before making his first volley. This permits the server to hit a much larger percentage of his first volleys offensively. That is, he can get in close enough to punch his volleys down, rather than being forced into hitting a soft volley up from his feet, or making a difficult half-volley. The play made by the server on this first volley is often responsible for the ultimate outcome of the point.

Also, the deep serve gives the net man valuable time to position himself to cover the return. Obviously, he has more chance to poach effectively with a deep serve. A shallow serve, on the other hand, permits the receiver to move in and knock the ball down the throat of the server's partner at net, at the feet of the server as he comes in, or sharply cross court for a placement. Besides, it is much easier for the receiver to lob offensively from close range. These points are illustrated in Figure 6.

In serving to the backhand court all the remarks about depth of

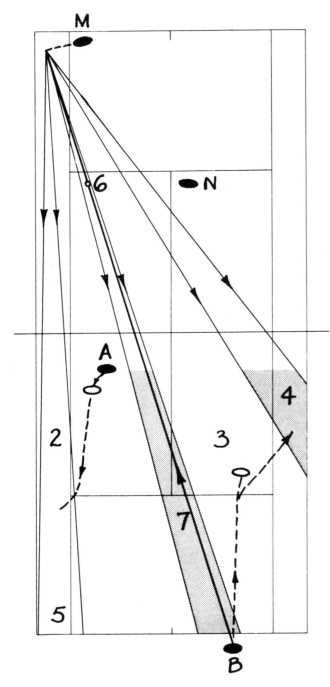

Figure 5

A slice serve to area 6 puts the serving team in an unenviable position. The partners face a strong forehand return and must guard wider angles of the court.

Net man **A** has to choose between dropping back and over a step to guard against a forehand drive down the alley (area 2), and moving slightly to the right to cover the center. The server **B** also has to anticipate the return. He must come up the center to protect the middle (areas 3 and 7) or move wide to protect against sharply angled shots to area 4. The angled shot can be hit harder than the dink in Figure 4. A topped drive can now be kept in the court; it passes over a lower portion of the net when hit sharply cross-court. This means the server does not have as much time to get up to net to protect area 4 as he did when serving to the backhand as in Figure 4. In addition, lobs hit to area 5 must be played on the weak backhand overhead by net man **A**.

Yes, a serve to area 6 means the serving team must anticipate the return unerringly in setting up the volleying offensive position, or the receiving team can hit through a hole for a placement or force a weak first volley.

service continue to hold. However, the rules for the forehand court, designed to minimize the angles of return, no longer apply. Now the serve generally should be placed in the backhand corner instead of the forehand corner in the center of the court. Here are the reasons why: (a) The great majority of tennis players are considerably less effective in playing the backhand stroke, more than offsetting the potential advantage of greater angles of return presented them. The high-bounding American twist service is especially difficult for a weak backhand. (b) The down-the-line return by the receiver, whether a drive or a lob, is less troublesome in the forehand court, since it is covered from the forehand side by the net man. (c) The receiver can ill afford to run around a well-placed serve to the backhand: he would end up way out of position for the next shot.

The slice and flat serves to the forehand corner are safer to use in the backhand court than in the forehand court because the angles of return are restricted. Therefore, these serves can be used with confidence to keep the receiver off balance. Experiment will help to determine the receiver's weakness. G. P. Hughes has written that after offering up a variety of serves to Don Budge in the backhand court and studying the effectiveness of return, he found that a serve hit directly at Budge gave him the best results. Remember that the server must feel out the weaknesses of the receiver much as a pitcher studies a batter in baseball.

The importance of teamwork begins to show just as soon as the ball is put into play and the serving team moves to position itself properly for the return of service.

The initial position of the net man, previously shown in Figure 3, is six to nine feet from the net and about one foot to the right of center of a line dividing the service courts and the sideline. The exact starting position of the net man depends on his height, reach, anticipation, and agility. In other words, his position is a function of his ability to cover his area and cope with the return of service, whether it be a dink shot, a drive, or a lob.

The net man must watch the service pass over the net and determine where it will land in the service court. A split-second later he should shift his attention from the ball to the receiver and try to anticipate from the receiver's stance and the manner in which he prepares to make his stroke where the return will go and what type of shot it will be—flat drive, top-spin drive, chop, angled-spin shot, or lob. A continuing study of his opponent's strokes and habits, coupled with the

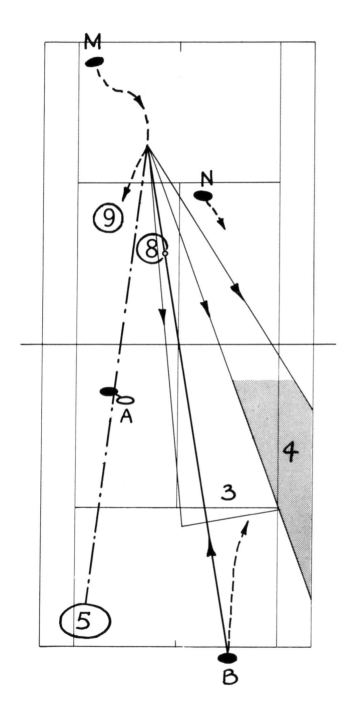

Figure 6

A shallow serve is likely to hand the offense to the receiving team. This diagram shows how. Receiver **M** moves in and runs around the serve bouncing at area 8, to pound it with his forehand and move in to net. Server **B** must hustle, but even so he cannot get in far enough to make an effective first volley. In fact, he cannot quite get to the service line. Thus receiver **M** can either play his shot at the vulnerable spot at the server's feet in area 3 or go for a possible placement in area 4, which the server does not have time to cover. Net man **A** must move a bit back and toward the center to defend against a ball hit through him at point-blank range, and to protect against a lob. Still he is unable to defend well against a disguised lob to area 5.

A shallow serve hit to area 9 is even worse, for the large angle and lobbing areas open to receiver **M** will almost certainly allow him to put the serving team in real trouble. In this case net man **A** would normally move to his left and back a step, and server **B** should come up wider and pray that he can get his racquet on the ball.

knowledge of where the serve is landing, should help the net man to anticipate quite accurately just what to expect for a return.

The net man is now ready to position himself. This involves a number of factors. Perhaps the most important of these is timing. No move, other than a fake, should be made until the receiver is fully committed to his shot. A premature start is likely to leave an opening for a placement. In fact, the interval of time between the anticipation and the move is extremely brief. It is that split second between the moment the receiver is sufficiently set so that he can no longer alter his shot, and the moment when the ball is struck. Raymond Little has put it aptly: "Half the art of anticipation is to conceal the fact that you have anticipated."

The next factor involved is the point at which the serve strikes in the service court. The net man's original stance puts him in the proper position to handle the return of a service landing mid-point of the width of the opponent's service court line. Thus, as a general rule, the net man holds his ground for the serve to the forehand court. If the serve is to preferred position 1 of Figure 4, he can afford to move a step toward the center at the proper moment to help protect the middle, and he can largely ignore the possibility of the difficult backhand shot down the alley. If the serve is to point 4, he should move a half-step to the left to cover up the alley. If the serve is both to the forehand and shallow, he should move back a step and a step toward the alley, for the receiver is almost on top of him for a drive down the alley. Moving back a step also helps to cover a lob that the receiver might hit cross-court to fool the server, who must close fast to cover the possibility of a sharp cross-court shot. The speed of the serve has an effect on the net man's position too, since the occasional fast serve permits him to take more chances and crowd the net or poach in expectation of a weak return. A slow, shallow serve should prompt the net man to move back a half-step, to get more time to volley the ball.

Because his forehand is on the sideline, the movement of the net man is slightly different when the serve goes to the backhand court. In general, the net man will hold his original position for a serve to the preferred point in the backhand corner, move a half-step to his left for a serve to the center, and move a full step toward the center for a serve to the forehand corner.

Finally, the net man has to position himself according to the type of return he anticipates. This, obviously, can upset the general positioning based on the bounce point of the serve. For example, let us suppose the receiver has given away his intention to hit down the alley by looking first in that direction, placing his feet, and setting himself for the shot. Then, regardless of bounce point, the net man should prepare himself by moving a half-step toward the alley at the proper moment. But, if the receiver is set to lob, the net man should move back a step and prepare to try to get the ball on his forehand overhead. This calls for the net man to move to his left in either court. By anticipating the speed of the return of service, and the depth from which it will be hit, the net man can judge what liberties to take in poaching. (More will be said about poaching later.) Continuous concentration by the net man should enable him to guess the enemy plans and win or save many points each set; but mental lapses and ill-timed moves can embarrass his partner and lose points as well.

Now let us return to the server, whom we left in the act of hitting the serve. Just after he hits the ball, he must bring his foot over the base line and start running for the net in a straight line in a series of quick, long steps. He must run on every serve until he is absolutely certain it is a fault. All too often a player halts his run toward the net when a serve looks as if it will be out, only to have it drop in safely. Then the receiving team returns one at his feet, takes the offensive away from him, and leaves him looking mighty foolish.

After following his serve straight in about four steps, depending on his length of stride, the server should be prepared to change direction to meet the situation. The change of direction should be made about a stride short of the service line. Some players actually bring both feet parallel to the net at this point, so that they can move in any direction with ease. The server, like the net man, should position himself according to the bounce point of his serve and his anticipation of the return of service. Since about 85 per cent of returns of service are hit at the incoming server, he must note quickly the approximate bounce point and then concentrate his attention not on the ball but on anticipating the receiver's type of return. Then he must move toward the proper area to intercept the return at a spot as close to the net as possible—about nine feet. The importance of getting in close has been illustrated in Figures 4, 5, and 6, and will become even more evident in Chapter VI.

Here again teamwork plays a strong part, for when the server sees the net man change position, he can change his position accordingly. The best average positions for over-all defense of several service bounce points have been shown in Figures 3, 4, 5, and 6. These are the positions the serving teams should occupy in preparing to handle the return of service.

A well-executed lob is particularly difficult for the server to handle, since he is moving forward rapidly to get in close to net; and a lob on second serve with the receiver in closer is even more difficult. Therefore the server must anticipate these shots and change direction a stride short of the service court. The net man must anticipate cross-court lobs so that he can cover for his partner when the server fails to anticipate and gets caught off balance.

Another bit of advice: you should familiarize yourself with the new foot fault rules and work hard to avoid breaking them. It is bad enough to take unfair advantage of one's opponents in a friendly match, when faults are usually not called. But in the heat of an important match it is heartbreaking to sprint for the net behind a beautiful serve, all prepared to smash a return—and then have the judge call a foot fault. It has happened at critical points in many a match, and its upsetting influence has been blamed for numerous defeats.

Unconventional Serving Formations

Two axioms of the sporting world—keep the opponents off balance and change tactics if losing—are responsible for the birth of the unconventional stratagem in every game. It is only logical that surprise changes of defense should become important elements in the game of doubles.

Near the turn of the century both the Americans and the Australians experimented with a reverse formation for the serving team. The practice of placing the net man on the same side of the court of the server (shown in Figure 7) was designed to offset an outstanding cross-court return of service. In other words, the server just got very tired of digging beautifully placed returns of service out of the turf and losing many points as a result of his weak first volleys. Instead of despairing or losing his temper (as too many of our younger players seem to do), he decided to change tactics and try a new formation. There are two reasons why this made good sense. First, the net man can take up the best defensive position against the return of service, and not be forced to move very far to make the volley. Second, the receiver, faced with an offsetting defense for his practiced return, is usually less effective whenever he elects to play down the line at the server coming up the reverse side.

Properly executed, unconventional serving formations can be most disconcerting to the opponents. With the variety of formations, poaches, and fakes used against him, the receiver can literally be

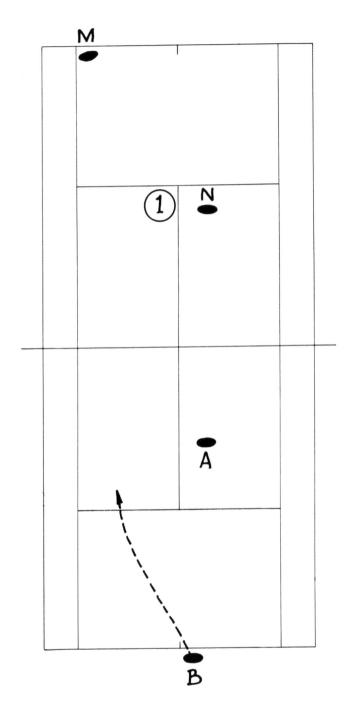

Figure 7

This illustrates the reverse formation of the serving team, used against an opponent having an outstanding cross-court return of service. The play is more difficult for the server when serving from the right side, as he may be forced to run far to make a backhand volley. For this reason the server must keep his serve near the center aim point 1 to prevent an offensive return of service down the alley. Note that the server positions himself near the center of the court in order to minimize the distance he must cover to reach his net position.

When using this type of formation to serve to the backhand court, the service can be placed down the middle to minimize the angle of return or to the usual backhand corner spot. It is safe in this instance to serve wide because the offensive backhand return down the line is more difficult to make, and server **B** has the easier forehand volley to play.

This diagram shows the surprise poach and the signaled poach.

In the surprise poach net man **A** is on his own. He usually chooses to poach on a fast service to aim point 1, which usually forces a weak or high return of service. He must time his start to coincide with the moment receiver **M** is committed, or the receiver will note his move and slip one down the line for an easy placement. Server **B** follows his service straight in to net in the normal manner until he notes the poach; then he veers to left or right on path 2 or 3 to cover the court.

In the signaled poach the server knows that because the net man will move he should go straight in for two steps, then cut left along path 4 to cover the backhand side. If server **B** starts to move to his left too soon, as shown in path 5, it gives away the poach to receiver **M** and allows him time to change his return and hit it down the line for the point.

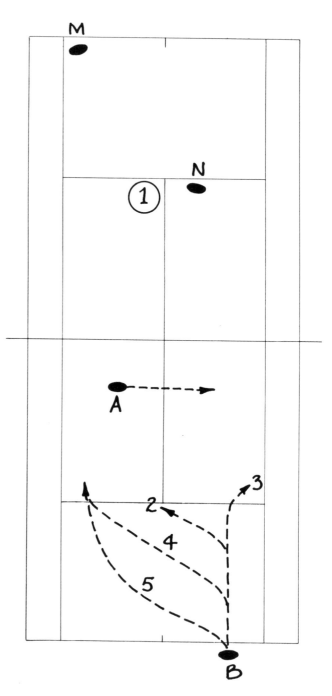

Figure 8

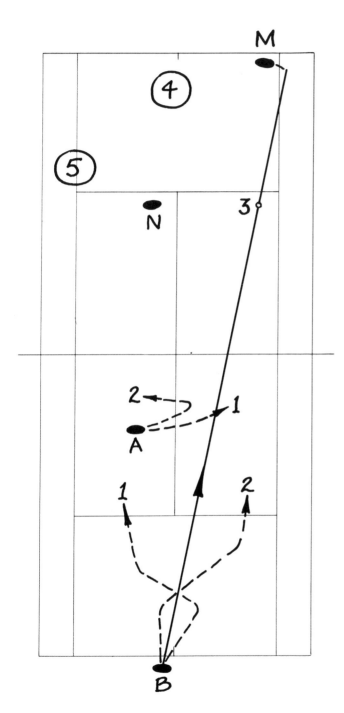

Figure 9

Two fakes are possible from the reverse serving formation.

In case 1, server **B** serves to the backhand corner (aim point 3) and fakes beautifully by starting up the right side on path 1. Net man **A** holds his position until receiver **M** is committed and then poaches rapidly along path 1 in hopes that he can volley the return of service diagonally to aim point 4 for the point.

In case 2, net man **A** starts his poach along path 2 while server **B** keeps the fake authentic by moving in straight along path 2 before cutting to the right. Net man **A**, having drawn a cross-court return by receiver **M**, reverses his field along path 2 in the hope he can volley easily to aim point 5 for the point.

This diagram shows two fakes from the conventional serving formation.

In the first case the serve is hit to aim point 3. The net man fakes a poach by starting early along path 1, while the server **B** continues the fake by moving to his left before cutting to the right along path 1. Then net man **A** moves rapidly to his left to volley the down-the-line return he has drawn to aim point 4 for the point.

In the second case the serve is hit to aim point 5 and net man **A** moves ahead of schedule to his left to cover the down-the-line return and draw a cross-court return. Meanwhile server **B** moves straight in as usual to carry out his deception before swerving to his left along path 2. Then, at the proper moment, net man **A** poaches rapidly to his right along path 2 and volleys the cross-court return to aim point 6 for the point.

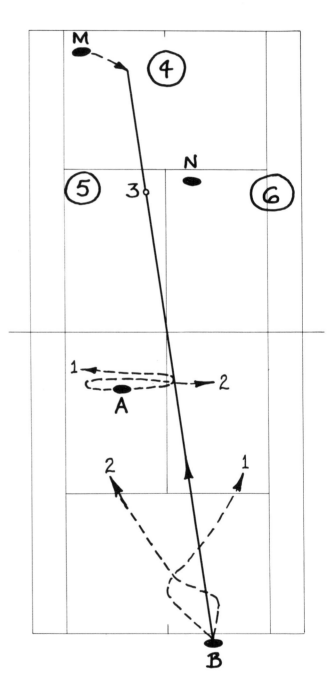

Figure 10

driven to distraction. The receiver is forced by such tactics to watch the movements of the serving team, as well as the ball, until the last split-second, so that he is more likely to err. In the 1954 National Doubles several teams used well-practiced unconventional formations to advantage. In general, the plays were triggered by signals set up before the point as the net man turned his back to the net and faced the server. Variety in play was the keynote. Figures 7, 8, 9, and 10 show some of the permutations and combinations. Note that there are several fake plays possible from each formation.

Unconventional formations and fakes require the partners to practice signals and timing. Nothing makes a team feel more foolish than to pull a tricky maneuver and have it backfire. For example, one of the authors played a match in the late afternoon against a team which had this poaching maneuver: the server came up the reverse side whenever the net man signaled a poach by scratching his back. This particular evening the gnats were not only out in force but biting savagely. Unfortunately the net man often forgot himself and scratched vigorously at frequent intervals. This was so confusing to the server that in the first set many points were lost as one whole side of the court was left unguarded. Happily, the humor of the situation saved the scratching team, and it went on to win.

CHAPTER V

The Return of Service

The return of service is considered by many the most important single shot in doubles, since, even if you win all your services, you must break through the opponent's serve at least once to win a set. The return of service is certainly the most difficult shot to play both consistently and effectively. If you doubt it, just consider how seldom service breaks are engineered in good doubles. An average championship match has only about one service break in seven games, and many times a particularly good server will go for a long stretch without losing his delivery. For example, Rex Hartwig won his service thirty-seven consecutive times in capturing the United States title in 1953! Hartwig's record and others like it are largely the receiver's responsibility, since it is the quality of his return of service that determines the tactics of the defensive team and the offensive team at the start of each point. Table VI notes dramatically the low relative potency of the return of service.

As he lines up, the receiver should bear three objectives in mind. First and foremost he must return the service. No one ever won a point by failing to return service, and many a point has been won on the worst of returns because even the best of opponents will err. (In fact, almost half the points won on successful returns of service are due to errors by the serving team!) Forcing the other team to *win* the point is a must. Second, the receiver should try to make a return that will allow his team to take the offensive or to gain the net position safely. Third, he should make his way to the net at the earliest possible opportunity. This is easy to say, but not easy to do.

Actually, the receiver is in a terrible predicament. There he is, facing a bruiser who hits a slow, high-bounding twist service to his weak backhand. The server then comes bounding in to the net where he joins his partner. They look like two snarling giants. (Stoefen actually was built along the lines of a pro basketball center.) The poor receiver has to keep an eye on the ball in order to be able to hit it, an eye on the net man to see if he is planning to poach, and an eye on the server to see where he is positioning himself. This with only two eyes! On top of all that, he has to make a split-second decision on the type of shot he will hit and where he will endeavor to place it. The problems and pressures are so great that the control displayed by the expert doubles player is little short of miraculous. Data taken on John Bromwich in championship play showed that in two matches he failed to return only twenty-one services in one hundred games, for a batting average of over .900! The usual batting average of successful returns is nearer .800 for championship and good club play.

The proper initial positions for the receiving team are shown in Figure 11. Note that the receiver is just inside the base line, or more accurately, as close in as he dares. His partner is at a modified net position just inside the service line and nearer the center of the court than the sidelines.

As mentioned in Chapter II, this formation was introduced by the famous Doherty brothers about 1903. Yet in the intervening fifty-odd years the practicality of their idea has failed to dawn on many tennis players of the first rank. The Australians saw the value of the formation in 1906 and have used it exclusively ever since in their rise to doubles supremacy. But in this country the noted tennis writers condemned it, and as late as 1928 even our Davis Cup doubles team was still using the weak, two-men-back-on-the-base-line receiving position. This is astounding when analysis indicates clearly that the Doherty formation gives the receiving team a much better chance to break service, as it permits them to move more readily in to the attacking position at net. In effect, the Americans condemned the formation because our stars did not have adequate returns of service—and the effectiveness of the Doherty formation depends on a *good* return of service! The old axiom still rings true: the best defense is a good offense—or at least a strong counterattack.

In 1924 Tilden let go a blast at the American receiving formation: "The first method of meeting this attack [serve] is with both receivers standing back on the base line. Under this system, the man returning service merely puts the ball in play, allowing the server a compara-

Receiver **M** should stand a step or two inside the base line, depending on the strength of the serve he faces. He should stand, as shown, on a line drawn (3) from the server through a point in the middle of the deep portion of the service court so that he can cover a serve to either corner.

The advantages of the cross-court return of service to area 4 are obvious from the diagram. Net man **A** is already in position to intercept close to the net a return within his reach and volley it offensively. On the other hand, as receiver **M** is about to stroke his return, server **B** has only reached point 1, or thereabouts, on his journey to the net. Thus the entire cross-court area is safe for a good return. Since server **B** is able to get in only as far as about point 2 by the time the cross-court return arrives, the receiver still has a chance to place the ball at his feet and force the server to hit up a weak defensive volley.

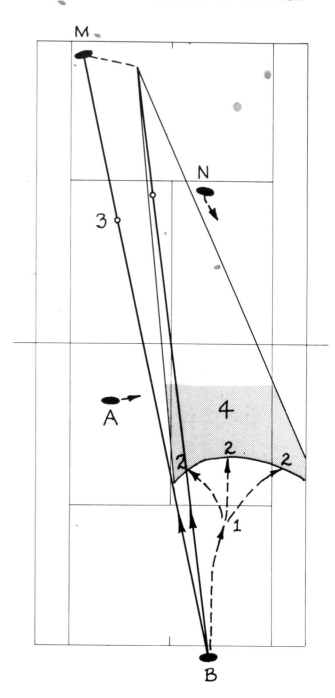

Figure 11

tively easy volley, and the attempt to win the point or obtain the offensive comes after this volley. In other words, it is the third or fourth shot that really starts the offensive of the receivers. This plan is the American style of doubles, and is largely responsible for our lack of first-class doubles teams in the United States."

Table IV shows that about 30 per cent of all strokes in doubles are returns of service. Many types of shots are employed, including the flat drive, topped drive, dink shot, offensive lob, and defensive lob. To determine the frequency of these strokes and the directions in which the experts hit them, complete data were taken on the contestants in the first three sets of the finals of the 1950 National Doubles at Longwood. These data and others are recorded in Table IX.

Most striking in Table IX is the heavy preponderance of cross-court returns used by the experts. Actually 114 of the 122 returns, or 93 per cent, were cross-court. Note also that only six lobs were hit in the championship match. The table also shows clearly which types of returns permitted the receiver to follow the shot into the net. The types of returns that produced winning points, directly or indirectly, are shown in Table X. The 1952 U. S. National Doubles Championship between Rose and Seixas and Sedgman and McGregor was monitored for this information; it was an exciting match won by Rose and Seixas 3-6, 10-8, 10-8, 6-8, 8-6.

Let us turn now to the receiver and consider his position, the position of the serving team, types of strokes, aim points for returns, and team play.

In positioning himself, the receiver should think first of time. After delivery of the service every split second favors the server, as it permits him to get in closer to the net and gain an offensive volleying position. To obtain an advantage the receiver must force the server to hit a defensive volley—that is, a volley hit up from below the level of the net. The receiver should try first to return service so as to prevent the server from making a deep offensive volley. He should stand in as close as possible and try to return the service quickly at the feet of the server as he advances. This means the more expert players should try to take the ball on the rise. If the ball is caught on the rise, the American twist serve, which takes a wicked bound, will not pull the receiver way out of position. (Budge was noted for his ability to receive this type of service in close and crack the ball with his famous backhand at the server's feet.) The closer in the receiver, the better his opportunity to hit his cross-court return at a sharp angle: he has that much more of

TABLE IX

RETURNS OF SERVICE

Final Round U. S. National Doubles Championship 1950

| | Cross Court | | | | Down Line | | | Cross Court | | | | Down Line | |
	Flat Drive	Topped Drive	Dink Shot	Lob	Drive	Lob		Flat Drive	Topped Drive	Dink Shot	Lob	Drive	Lob
Player	Bromwich (forehand court)							Talbert (forehand court)					
Total number	17	7	7	0	0	2		9	2	17	0	0	0
Number followed in to net	4	5	7	0	0	0		0	0	5	0	0	0
Player	Sedgman (backhand court)							Mulloy (backhand court)					
Total number	12	13	2	0	1	0		10	4	14	0	1	1
Number followed in to net	2	12	1	0	0	0		0	2	4	0	0	0

TYPES OF RETURNS OF SERVICE

Composite Data from Several Matches During the Same Tournament

| | Cross Court | | | | Down Line | | |
	Flat Drive	Topped Drive	Dink Shot	Lob	Drive	Dink Shot	Lob
Forehand No.	34	23	51	0	2	3	15
Court %	27	18	40	0	1	2	12
Backhand No.	33	27	51	1	3	2	14
Court %	25	21	39	1	2	1	11

TABLE X

TYPES OF RETURNS OF SERVICE ON POINTS WON BY RECEIVING TEAM, INCLUDING DATA ON RETURNS FOLLOWED IN TO NET BY RECEIVER

| | Drive | | | Dink | | | Top Spin | | | Slice | | | Lob | | |
	No. Winners	Took Net	No Approach	No. Winners	Took Net	No Approach	No. Winners	Took Net	No Approach	No. Winners	Took Net	No Approach	No. Winners	Took Net	No Approach
Sedgman and McGregor	21	3	18	14	8	6	8	7	1	9	3	6	0	0	0
Rose and Seixas	10	2	8	15	12	3	12	1	11	4	0	4	5	2	3

a head start in following the return to net; and he needs the head start, since he is the last of the four players to reach the net.

In point of actual position the receiver, on first serve, should stand a foot or more inside the base line, on a line drawn from the server through the center of the service courts (Figure 11). The exact distance he stands inside the base line depends on the speed of the serve and his own reach and reaction time. He should remember that the server in doubles can afford only rarely to go for the ace; and from time to time he should play in closer to tease the server into single or double faults in trying for aces. Often a server can be upset by a receiver who "rolls" with the serve. (Rolling is a move to run around the serve as the ball is thrown up by the server. The maneuver is designed to catch the server's eye and cause him to hurry or to try to change direction of the serve.) Anticipation helps to determine the best position for the receiver. He should study the server carefully: most players give away their serve by the toss, stance, or backswing. Thus, the receiver can move up or back, or be prepared to run around the serve, depending on his ability to anticipate. Many of the topflight players consistently anticipate and run around serves that are not hit too far over on the backhand, in order to take them on the stronger forehand side. It is not safe to run around serves hit well into the backhand corner. It puts the receiver too far out of position and opens up the court to his opponent's first volley (see Figure 38).

The receiver should move in about one or two steps to play a second serve. Even though the second serve in championship doubles is almost as fast as the first, the receiver can afford to gamble that the server will not go for the ace. Again, statistics showed the second service to rank last in lethality. The receiving team has almost twice as good a chance to win the point on second as on first service. The receiver can play the ball earlier, which gives him the opportunity to make an offensive shot at the feet of the server; and he can get to the net quicker to cut off the return volley. Every step forward provides an extra advantage! In club doubles, where the receiver often encounters a weak second serve, he must move well in and capitalize on his offensive return and an easy excursion to the net.

What is the formation of serving team confronting the receiver? Figure 11 illustrates the average position after a good first service. Note that the net man has taken advantage of the bounce point of the serve (see Chapter IV) and has moved over a step toward the center. The server has also taken advantage of this—has come up a bit wide and reached a point about one step inside the service line, where, as he continues to move in, he is ready to move in any direction to volley the return. The good court coverage here shows the phenomenal accuracy required of the return of service if it is to have a chance of gaining the offensive for the receiving team. Figure 11 proves conclusively that the best single shot for the receiver is cross-court at the inrushing server, which explains why 93 per cent of the returns of service (see Table IX) were cross-court.

There are several strokes which can be used to return service cross-court to the aim point areas in Figure 12. Although the type of stroke differs with the individual and the serve delivered, its purpose in all cases should be the same: to force the server (or a poaching net man) to volley up or make a defensive volley. Keep the return low. If it comes in too high, the server will powder it down for a placement. Keep the ball low! We had this important principle driven home strongly one day in a close match at Longwood involving Bromwich and Sidwell against Gonzales and Parker. To the untrained eye it appeared that Parker had played his return of service exceptionally well, and had made very few errors in losing a close match. In fact, in one twenty-four-game set he failed to return service only twice! Yet, in the shower room after the match Bromwich, the old master, had only one comment to make to Parker: "Tough luck, Frankie. Your backhand return of service was coming in a bit high today."

The popularity and effectiveness of the cross-court return of service have a purely mechanical basis. The net in tennis is six inches lower at the center than at the sideline, so that it is obviously easier to execute a lower stroke cross-court over the middle of the net.

There are two returns of service which permit the receiver to keep the ball low and force the receiver to volley up. These are the dink shot (a distant cousin to the drop shot) and the topped drive, rated as the two best returns of service in doubles.

First introduced by Beals Wright near the turn of the century, the dink shot return of service has been brought to perfection by Lott and Bromwich. This soft chop or slice shot is hit well within the service court, usually at a wide angle cross-court. When hit with crazy spin off the two-fisted forehand of Bromwich or the delicate undersliced backhand of Jack Crawford, the dink will drive the server wild trying to volley it accurately. To add to the server's dink-inspired woes, he must sprint way in to the net to get to the ball, and then he practically has to dig a divot in the court to volley it. If the server slows down to try to take it on the bounce, the receiver can take advantage by mixing up his returns and hitting drives at the server's feet.

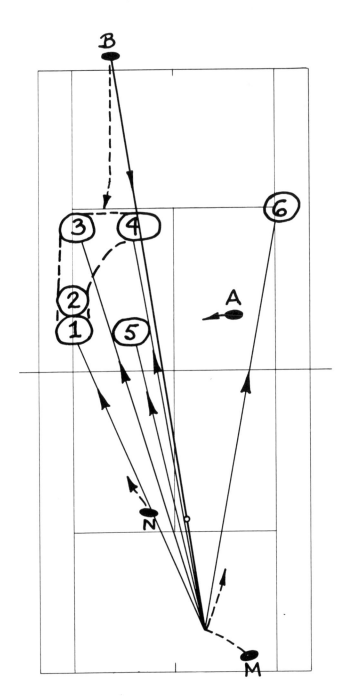

This diagram shows the preferred target areas for returns of service when the receiver is facing the most difficult serving situation, namely a twist service to the backhand corner. Note that net man **A** has taken advantage of the bounce point of the serve and moved toward the center. This leaves receiver **M** with a very limited area for his return. His best shots are a dink to area 1, topped drive to area 2, or a drive to area 3 or 4. Also effective is a dink or topped drive slipped through the center, out of reach of net man **A**, to aim point 5. A drive to area 6 is possible only if net man **A** has moved too far to the center, or has started to poach too soon.

Approximately 80 per cent of all returns should fall in the dotted areas. The shallow returns to areas 1 and 2 are preferred because they should force server **B** to volley up defensively. Note that receiver **M** is running to the net to try to gain an offensive position. His path is wide in anticipation of a cross-court return volley by server **B**.

Figure 12

Besides forcing the server to volley up, the dink shot has three other advantages. First, it is a safe shot which enables the receiver to put the ball consistently into play. Second, it prevents the server from getting much pace on his volley. And third, it is a slow, spinning shot that gives the receiver extra time to get in to the net. (See Tables IX and X. Here Bromwich got in behind every dink he hit, and the dink was the only return of service Talbert could follow in.) The only hitch is that the dink is somewhat hard to make off the cannonball serve the receiver is occasionally called upon to face.

The second-best return of service is the severe top-spin stroke, called the topped cross-court drive. It has been used with telling effect by such excellent receivers as Sedgman and Van Ryn. It has all the assets of the dink shot but one. It is safe, and it forces the server to volley the ball up—though with a little more pace than he can get on the dink shot. However, it does not give the receiver quite as much time to get in to the net: its travel time is shorter than that of the dink shot so it is volleyed sooner. (See Tables IX and X.) Note that Bromwich and Sedgman were very successful in coming to net behind the topped-drive return. In fact, they made it 85 per cent of the time.

Ranking third among recommended returns of service is the flat drive hit cross-court. Its principal application is to win points outright by forcing errors or by making placements (as shown in Table X). It is most effective against a fast serve, since the receiver can often return the ball swiftly enough to catch the server near the service line and force him to volley up from this point or play a tricky half-volley. Against a fast serve the drive need not be too low. Played safely *well above the net,* it will still catch the server in deep court. (The drive was Little Bill Johnston's famous shot. Other great drivers were Tilden, Vines, and Perry.) The drawbacks of the flat drive are two: it is not as safe as the dink or topped cross-court drive, and it leaves the receiver less time to follow in behind. Tables IX and X show that the Americans were never able to follow in behind their flat drives; while the Australians were able to do so only approximately 21 per cent of the time. This is particularly significant when one considers Sedgman's great speed of foot.

Table IX also presents data on types of returns of service in eight sets of doubles play from three different matches during the semi-finals and finals at Longwood in 1950. The popularity of the cross-court dink, topped drive, and flat drive are once again clearly evident. Actually, 86 per cent of all returns were hit cross-court at the advancing server in the hope of drawing a weak first volley. Rarely are the three most effective returns of service hit down the line, where they would open up the opportunity for the alert net man to make a placement to the open diagonal area. When they are played, down-the-line returns of service are check shots, designed to keep the opposing net man "honest" and prevent him from doing too much poaching. The value of an occasional down-the-line shot should not be overlooked. It can often be turned into a placement—especially if the shot is to the corner off a service hit too wide in the forehand court, and the net man either fails to step toward the sideline to cover or starts to poach a split second too soon. Allison and Van Ryn often employed the strategy of playing a few drives down the line early in a match to discourage the net man from promiscuous poaching. Seixas and Trabert also used it effectively against Hoad and Rosewall in the 1954 National Doubles final.

The desirable aim points for return of service depend on the bounce point of the serve in the two service courts. Figures 12 through 17 cover the situation rather thoroughly. Do not forget that variety and deception are the spice of the game, and that the receiver should mix up his returns to keep the serving team off balance.

The fourth type of stroke for return of service is the lob. It was one of the most popular returns before the turn of the century. However, with the advent of the smashing style of overhead play, it became evident that the lob was too dangerous a return to be used with any regularity in championship play. There are really two distinct types of lobs used for returning service—one defensive, the other offensive. The defensive lob is used far more often.

Remembering that the receiver in doubles should stand inside the base line, as far in as he dares to take the service, you can see that server will catch him from time to time with a fast serve to the corner. The receiver, forced out of position, will generally have to scramble and to hit a weak defensive shot. A poor drive under these conditions can easily be intercepted and volleyed for a placement by the net man. Thus, the safest shot to play is a defensive lob (Figure 17). This type of lob should be hit high and deep. Table IX indicates that, of the 12 per cent of returns of service that are lobs, practically all are placed down the line in order to drive the net man back and upset the offensive position of the serving team. The lob must be high enough to give the receiver a chance to get back in position before the return is made, and to permit his partner at net time to shift his position if necessary. The positions they assume will depend on the effectiveness of the particular lob. If it appears the lob will be smashed, the receiver should try to run back to a spot about a yard behind the center of his portion

When the service is to the forehand corner, receiver **M** has a better chance to make an effective return because he is playing the return with his stronger forehand and has a larger area open to him. He can make a forehand drive down the line to aim point 5, so that net man **A** must move a half-step toward the alley to cover such a possibility. This opens up a greater area for the cross-court returns.

The preferred returns are the dink or topped drive to area 1. The topped drive can be played more shallow than shown in Figure 12 because the ball goes over a lower portion of the net. Played at such a wide angle, either shot should force server **B** to scramble for the ball, and will almost invariably cause him to make a defensive volley. Also the receiver has more room to hit the dink or topped drive to aim point 2, or the drive to aim point 4. A drive to aim point 3 is effective if the server is slow in moving to the net.

Area 81 is stuck in to show the aim point when playing against a man 81 years old, or a server who is too lazy to follow his serve into the net.

About 80 per cent of the returns of service will fall in the dotted areas.

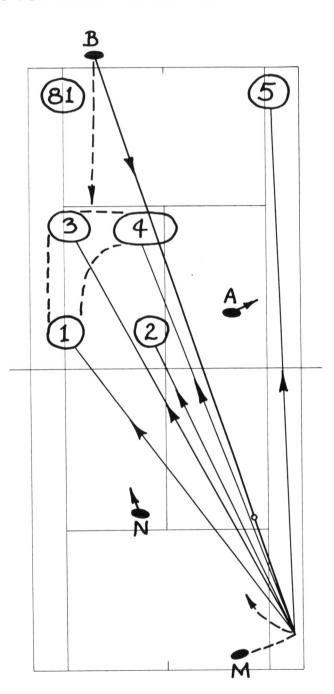

Figure 13

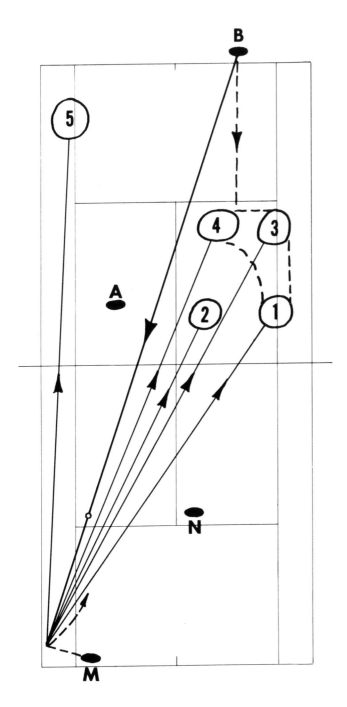

Here are the returns of serve recommended to receiver **M** when he faces the twist serve to the backhand corner of the backhand court. Net man **A** holds his position because the backhand drive return down the line is difficult to hit with sufficient speed to reach area 5 safely. The receiver should keep his backhand drive returns to area 4 away from the center of the court lest the net man have time to intercept the slower shots.

The most effective returns are dink shots and topped drives to aim point 1: they force server **B** to run a long distance and then play a difficult backhand volley up from close to the ground. To mix up the server occasional changes of pace (such as drives to area 3 or 4), or changes of direction (such as dinks or topped drives to area 2), should be employed.

Figure 14

A serve to the forehand corner of the backhand court opens up areas of return beyond those shown in Figure 14—despite the fact that net man **A** moves to cover the center. Greater speed off the forehand permits receiver **M** to drive down the center to aim point 4.

The recommended returns in this situation are the dink to area 1 and the topped drive to area 2 (deeper than Figure 14 because of the height of the net). To keep server **B** guessing, the dink to area 5 and the drives to areas 3 and 4 should be used. The drive to area 6 is practical only when net man **A** moves too far to the center or starts to poach prematurely.

Note again that the receiver persists in following his return in to net. In coming up wide he anticipates a cross-court volley return by server **B**.

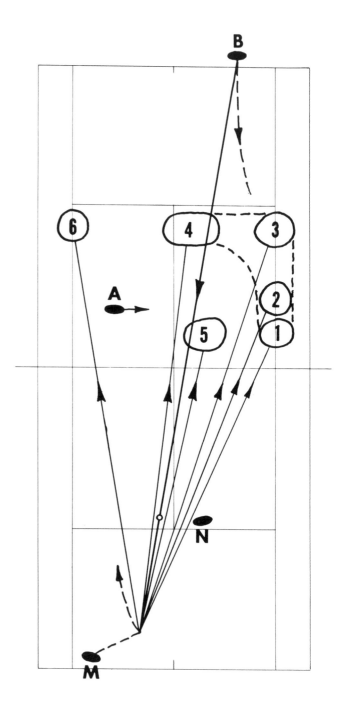

Figure 15

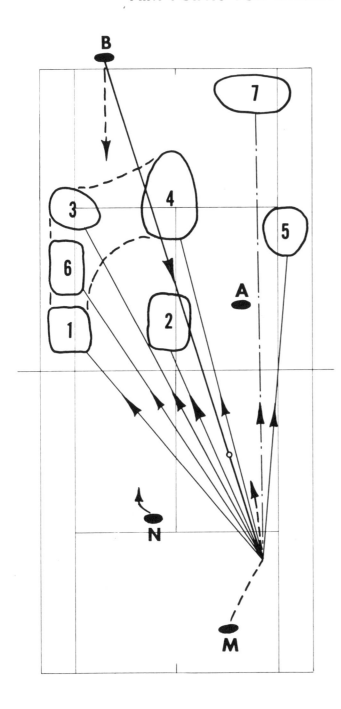

The shallow serve, whether to the forehand or backhand court, is a receiver's delight.

Receiver **M** should move up on the serve (as shown) to take the ball as soon as possible. This gives him a wider area of return because: (1) server **B** will not have had time to get in as far as the service line before the return is completed; and (2) because net man **A** dare not move to cover the center and risk a drive blasted by him from close range to aim point 5.

The preferred returns under these circumstances are drives and topped drives to area 6; they may result in placements if not anticipated unerringly by server **B**. The dink or topped drive to area 1 is next best. If the server starts up to net wide the receiver should pound a drive down the middle to aim point 4 or hit the dink or topped drive to aim point 2. If the server comes up near the middle a drive to aim point 3 should draw a weak return volley. A lob to area 7 becomes an easy shot for **M** from his close-in position.

Note that the receiver must follow in to net behind his return in order to take proper advantage of his offensive return of service.

Figure 16

If receiver **M** is caught off balance and forced to scramble for a fast serve to either corner, he might hit a poor return; so his best bet is a high defensive lob. The preferred shot is down the line to aim point 1: it has a chance of embarrassing the serving team by forcing net man **A** to retreat, whereas a high lob hit cross-court should be easy for server **B** to smash merely by halting his journey to the net and waiting for the ball.

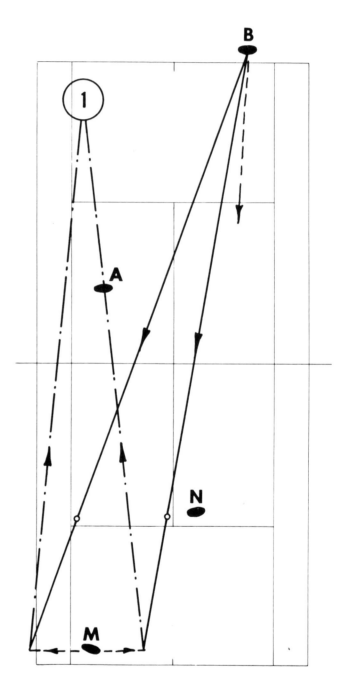

Figure 17

of the base line. If the lob is sufficiently high and deep, and the net man lets it bounce, the receiver may be able to get in to his proper position at net. Meanwhile, the receiver's partner at modified net position should, as a rule, hold his ground; but if the lob is quite short, he may elect to scurry back to a point a short distance beyond the center of his portion of the base line. He should, above all, try not to get caught in transit in the area between the service and the base lines, for he has a better chance to volley or hit a ground stroke than to half-volley a smash.

The offensive lob on the return of service is one of the most delicate shots in tennis. For this reason it is seldom used on anything but a weak, shallow serve—except by the masters of the lob, such as George Lott. By hitting a low, rather fast lob just over the head of the opposition, the receiver can reach an offensive position at net. But if the lob is too high, the opponents will have time to fall back and smash it; and if it is too low, they will knock it down your throat. Lott used to mask the shot beautifully by first faking a dink or drive, than catching the net man or the server by surprise. He and Brugnon hit the shot with top spin, so that it would bound away, beyond the reach of the opponents, for a placement. The offensive lob works best under one or more of the following circumstances:

1. When the serve is shallow and weak.
2. When the net man is crowding the net or is short in stature.
3. When the net man starts to poach early and is off balance as a result.
4. When the server is rushing the net so fast that he cannot reverse direction easily. Before playing the lob over the server's head, the receiver should move back a step to delay his return until the inrushing server is on top of the net.

Figure 18 shows the aim points for the various lobs.

In back-yard doubles the offensive lob can be used more often because the second serve is liable to be weak. Furthermore, any overhead played from deep court is usually much less dangerous when made by the less-than-expert opponent. In fact, the lob is still a basic return for the week-ender.

Variety and surprise are indispensable functions of the receiver's game. The receiver should be able to hit all types of returns of service and, at the same time, hide his intentions until the last second. Concealment had much to do with the success of Lott and Bromwich as doubles players. They started many of their strokes with the same motion, so that the type, direction, and speed of the shot were most diffi-

Shallow serves permit the receiver to add another offensive stroke to his repertoire—the low, fast offensive lob. Played after faking a dink or drive, it can often score a placement, particularly if hit with some top spin. Generally offensive lobs should be played over the backhand side of the net man to aim point 1. Sometimes there is a hole between players of the serving team, so that aim point 3 can be used. Area 2 is a beautiful aim point if the server has a habit of rushing to net so fast that he cannot put on the brakes and shift into reverse. On a slippery court such a lob can be most disconcerting to the server.

But a note of warning! Receiver **M** is supposed to follow his return in to the net; and if his lob is hit too low or if his intentions are anticipated by net man **A**, the poor receiver can be mortally wounded by an overhead smash.

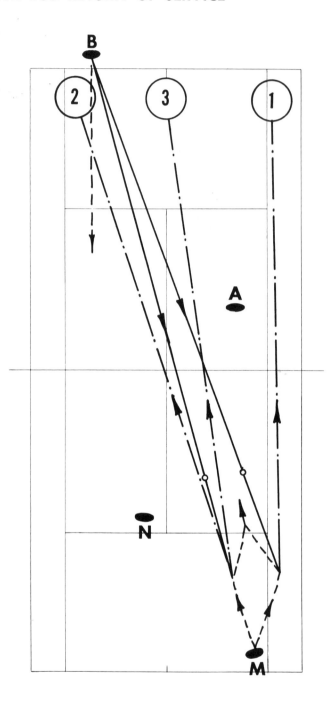

Figure 18

cult to anticipate. Concealment keeps the serving team off balance and helps to draw the weak volleys which lead to service breaks. It also makes effective poaching by the opposing net man much more difficult. A keen net man will study his opponents' style for various types of returns; in a short time he will have spotted certain "tipoffs"—gestures and mannerisms that help him poach effectively and turn good returns into placements. Not only must the receiver mask and vary his return of service, but he must also develop the habit of keeping an eye on the net man's movements while executing the return.

Like the server, the receiver must follow his shot in to the net position. To prove just how basic is this principle, data were collected on the number of points won and lost when the return of service was, and was not, followed in to the net. When an ace was served or the receiver made an error the point was ignored, since obviously the receiver had no chance to move in to the net, even if he wanted to. The data covered over a thousand points from fourteen matches, and included all types of servers and receivers. The figures (see Table XII) are startling.

While the serving team wins approximately 70 per cent of all points, and 64 per cent of all points where a successful return of service is made, *the receiving team wins 50 per cent of those returns followed in to net!* Surely these percentages are conclusive. If the receiver can stand in and hit the dink or topped-drive type of return—if he can force the server to volley up while dashing in to the net—he has a good, solid chance to win the point. It should be possible to follow in on 30 per cent of the successful returns of service, and occasionally the real experts will follow in 50 per cent. The chances of advancing to the net behind the return are six times greater on the second service, largely because the wise receiver moves in one or two steps and gets a big jump on the server. Followed returns, whether on first or second serve, are the stock-in-trade of championship doubles teams. As much as any single maneuver they made Lott, Bromwich, Van Ryn, and Sedgman outstanding. Coupled with the use of the Doherty formation (the partner of the receiver at modified net position), they have been largely responsible for the overwhelming success of Australian doubles teams.

Let us consider now the role of the receiver's partner. Since the receiving team in doubles will usually lose the game unless it manages to take the offense, the partner of the receiver is placed in a modified net position **N**, as shown in Figure 11, rather than on the base line. The advantages offered by this position will soon become evident.

The modified net man should base his play on three rules:

TABLE XI

RECEIVER VERSUS SERVER

Receiving Player	Receiving Team									Serving Team — Types of First Volleys Used by Serving Team (Numbers show final outcome of points on which such volleys were used.)															Servers
	Points Won				Points Lost					Deep		Semi-deep		Shallow		Angled		Down line		Hit up		Over-head		TOTALS against receivers		
	Return of service	Second shot	Third or subsequent shot	TOTALS	Error on return of service	First volley	Second shot	Third or subsequent shot	TOTALS	Won	Lost	Won	Lost	Won	Lost	Won	Lost	Won	Lost	Won	Lost	Won	Lost	Won	Lost	
Seixas	15	7	3	25	30	9	10	7	56	5	1	5	5	3	0	4	0	5	0	1	3	0	0	23	9	Hartwig and Fraser
Trabert	13	6	5	24	18	13	10	7	48	10	3	4	1	4	2	2	0	3	1	1	1	1	0	25	8	
TOTALS	28	13	8	49	48	22	20	14	104	15	4	9	6	7	2	6	0	8	1	2	4	1	0	48	17	
Hartwig	12	12	4	28	27	21	7	5	60	10	3	8	3	4	4	2	0	5	3	1	3	1	0	31	16	Seixas and Trabert
Fraser	16	6	2	24	25	11	8	4	48	5	4	3	3	0	1	2	2	8	0	0	0	1	0	19	10	
TOTALS	28	18	6	52	52	32	15	9	108	15	7	11	6	4	5	4	2	13	3	1	3	2	0	50	26	
Hoad	11	7	4	22	10	10	8	3	31	13	3	2	1	0	1	2	2	2	1	1	2	1	0	21	10	Richardson and Talbert
Rosewall	8	2	4	14	15	10	6	2	33	5	2	2	0	1	0	6	2	2	0	0	1	0	0	16	5	
TOTALS	19	9	8	36	25	20	14	4	64	18	5	4	1	1	1	8	4	4	1	1	3	1	0	37	15	
Richardson	8	6	0	14	12	19	11	2	44	16	1	7	2	1	0	3	0	1	0	0	4	0	0	28	7	Hoad and Rosewall
Talbert	12	6	2	20	14	17	3	4	38	11	3	0	0	2	1	2	0	3	0	0	4	2	0	20	8	
TOTALS	20	12	2	34	26	36	14	6	82	27	4	7	2	3	1	5	0	4	0	1	8	2	0	48	15	

TABLE XII

ENGINEERING THE SERVICE BREAK

Importance of Receiver's Following Return of Service In to Net

(Table based on 1069 points of championship play)

Over-all per cent of points won by receiving team	Per cent of points won by receiving team when not able to follow return of service in to the net	Per cent of returns of service receiver is able to follow in to the net	Per cent of points won by receiving team when able to follow in to the net	Per cent of points won by receiving team when receiver follows return of service in to net
36	31	30	50	50

1. *He must anticipate.*

To the uninitiated player, it may seem at first that to play the modified net position is to flirt unnecessarily with death. After all, the opponents at net can slam any high ball right into your stomach with the speed and force of a Joe Louis left hand. Maybe the Doherty brothers shouldn't have invented this exposed front-line position!

Well, the risk isn't as great as it may seem. The modified net man can learn to anticipate the intentions of the opponents rather easily, and once he has learned he can not only defend himself effectively, but also take the offense quite often.

Anticipating in the modified net position is an easy routine. The player should stand slightly sideways to the net, facing toward the opposing net man, **A.** As the serve is hit, he should watch the ball only long enough to note the start of the return of the service. Then he will know reasonably well the type and direction of the return, and what to expect on the first volley of the serving team. Immediately, he should shift his attention *ahead* of the ball to opposing net man, **A.** By watching him for an instant, he can discover any intention of the net man to intercept the return. If it is apparent that the opposing net man will not play the shot, the modified net man should continue to turn his eyes and body *ahead* of the ball toward the advancing server, to learn his position and the type of volley he is getting set to play. Thus, a quick sweep of the court, from receiver to net man to advancing server, tells the modified net man who will make the first volley. Then he should study the man about to hit the volley to anticipate accurately the type and direction of the shot. If the club player finds that he cannot keep up with such speedy, complex action, he should skip watching the receiver and concentrate on whether or not the net man will play the shot. He can turn to watch the advancing server an instant later.

2. *He must play his position so as to take advantage of weak first volleys by the serving team.*

Remember, the receiving team must take the offensive if it is to break service, and the recommended returns of service all work toward this end. Also remember that it is difficult for the receiver to force a weak volley on his return of service. So it becomes imperative that the receiving team be in a position to exploit every poor first volley.

The position of modified net man, **N,** is selected in part for just this purpose. He is close enough to the net to move in rapidly and hit down a defensive first volley hit up by the serving team. He is located near the center of the court because the server, volleying a good return of service from close to the ground, will usually hit it cross-court over the lowest part of the net; and player **N** has only to move a few feet to intercept the shot. It is also possible for player **N** to reach a volley hit down the line—because down-the-line volleys are hit up somewhat to clear the high portion of the net, and rather softly, to keep them from sailing over the base line. Of course, the modified net man has to anticipate the direction of the server's first volley and get a good jump on the ball (just like a good shortstop in baseball).

Typical points won by an alert modified net man are shown in Figures 19 and 20. It is sound tennis for player **N** to take chances by edging toward the center and preparing to poach when his partner makes an effective return of service. The Australians, with their quick-on-the-trigger anticipation, are particularly adept at poaching for a kill. The exact position of the modified net player is determined by his reach, agility, powers of anticipation, and by the effectiveness of his partner's return of service. In 1954 the long, lanky Australians were standing way in at times—eight feet from the net and five feet from the center line—particularly on second serves.

Obviously the receiver, as he follows in behind an effective return of service, may also be in a position to put away for a placement a volley hit up by the server. He should generally come up a little wide (as shown in Figure 19) to cover the part of the net his partner cannot reach.

Up to this point all returns of service mentioned or diagramed have been based on the assumptions that the serving team is using the conventional formation (depicted in Figure 11), and that the server is following his service in to the net position in every case. Let us now consider the return of service against unconventional or trick serving formations.

To begin with, the receiver, as he prepares to execute his return, must keep one of his "several" eyes on the serving team in order to detect any rapid change in position. There are several formations and fakes he might have to face (illustrated in Figures 7, 8, 9, and 10). In general, these formations are calculated to rattle, confuse, or surprise the receiver; and they will succeed on all counts unless the receiver is alert and knows what counteraction to take. These formations can be met successfully; otherwise, an unconventional formation would quickly become *the* conventional formation. The proper counterattacks are shown in Figures 21, 22, 23, and 24.

The receiver's partner at net must always watch the opposing net

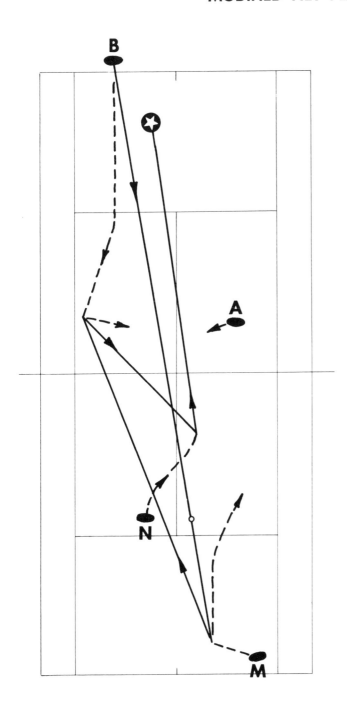

This diagram shows, in a perfect example of team play, why the modified net position has been accepted as the best position for the partner of the receiver.

Receiver **M** has hit a fine backhand cross-court dink, which forces server **B** to volley up from close to the net. Modified net player **N** has watched the cross-court return by receiver **M**. Then he notes that net man **A** is not planning a poach; that server **B** will reach the ball only after a long run; and, finally, that server **B** will volley up cross-court. Therefore, modified net man **N** moves a step or two toward the net on noting the low cross-court return of service, and then he dashes in to his right to cut off the anticipated cross-court defensive volley by server **B**. Thus he is able to poach and volley down the center for an easy placement.

Figure 19

This diagram shows the type of remarkable save an alert modified net player can make to win a point.

Receiver **M** makes a weak return, which permits net man **A** to move over and volley sharply at modified net player **N** for a seemingly easy point. But there is a hitch. Modified net player **N**, in surveying the action, has seen that net player **A** is about to intercept the poor return of service. Thus he is able to move to his left, anticipate the direction of net player **A**'s volley, and volley the shot back for a placement! This is the sort of play that can break the server's heart—and his service, too.

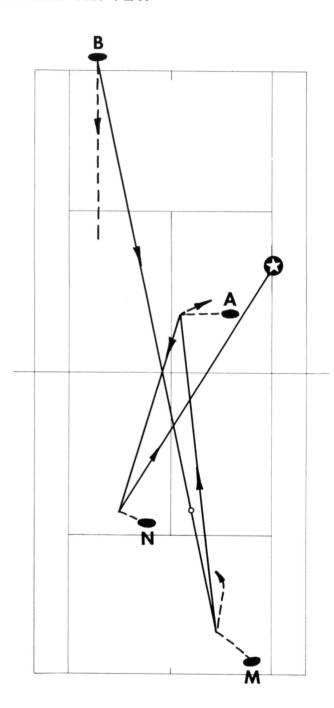

Figure 20

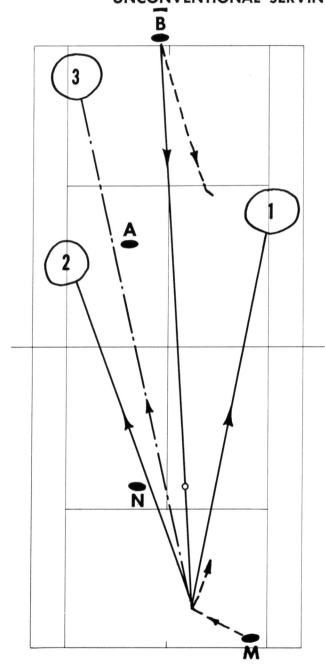

When the receiver faces the reverse serving formation in the forehand court, his best return is down the line to aim point 1. This will force server **B** to make a difficult running volley from a point low on his backhand. If net man **A** is too close to the center or back too far, a topped cross-court drive to area 2 is effective. If net man **A** is too close to the net, receiver **M** has the whole diagonal length of the court in his favor, and can play an offensive lob to aim point 3.

Essentially the same conditions hold for the receiver when the reverse formation is used in serving to the backhand court. Here, however, the down-the-line shot is somewhat easier for the server, who can reply effectively with a running forehand volley.

Figure 21

If receiver **M** has been having some success in playing the down-the-line return to aim point 1 (recommended in Figure 21) against the reverse serving formation, he should be alert for a planned poach play like the one pictured here. There is a simple counter: the instant receiver **M** sees net man **A** start his move, he should play the cross-court shot to area 2. With any luck it will gain him a point. A lob to aim point 3 is also an effective play.

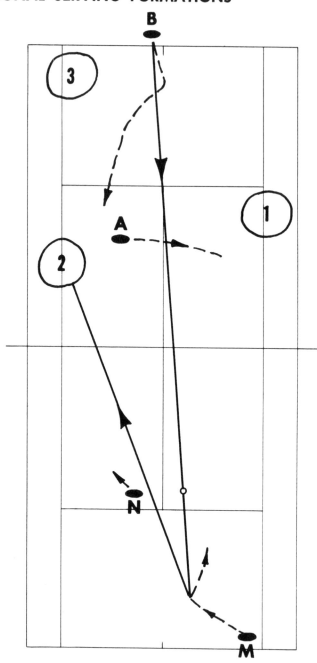

Figure 22

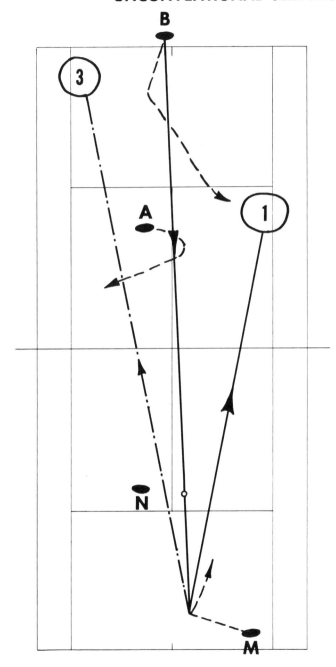

The receiver who has mastered the returns against the formations shown in Figures 21 and 22 still has another problem to face—the fake poach on the reverse serving formation. If receiver **M** is alert and his judgment sound, he can detect a fake poach from the course taken by either net man **A** or server **B**. He can ruin this maneuver by hitting down the line to aim point 1. Another effective return is the deep crosscourt lob to aim point 3.

Figure 23

This diagram depicts the ordinary poach play. It is used by the serving team when least expected, particularly when receiver **M** has been setting himself carefully and consistently playing effective cross-court returns. The proper counter: receiver **M** should play a low drive down the line.

Many wise doubles players make this type of return from time to time as a check play to keep net man **A** from promiscuous poaching. If the receiver keeps his shot low, net man **A** cannot do much more than volley it straight back. However, if the drive comes in too high, you can just about kiss the point good-by. The net man can volley it down severely through the open diagonal for a placement.

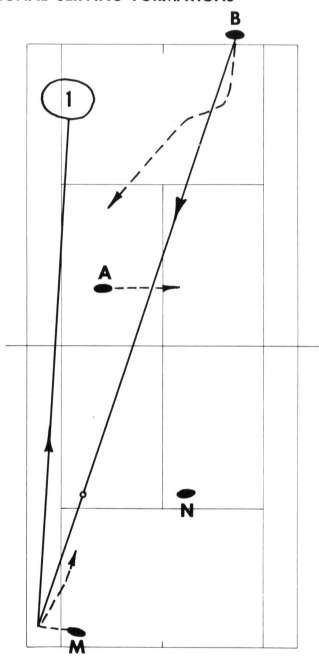

Figure 24

man carefully on a poach play. He should not close toward the net, but get set to make a defensive return of the poach, if possible.

If a server is thrown off balance, or is old, tired, or lazy, he may fail to follow his service in to the net. The alert receiver, immediately aware of the lapse, should alter his tactics to take maximum advantage of it. Here the dink and short-topped drive are not so effective: either shot would allow the server to correct his mistake by moving up to play a ground stroke from near the service line, where he could make an offensive shot and finally gain his proper position at net. Instead, the receiver should hit a deep cross-court drive, which will hold the server in the back court, and follow his drive rapidly in to the net. Other good strokes to use are sliced or chopped shots hit to an area deeper than the service court. Preferably these strokes should have a low bounce, so that the server is forced to dig them up for a weak return. Any one of these strokes will force a defensive return by the server; and with one man up and one back, the ranks of the serving team can be pierced through the open diagonal. This play (illustrated in Figure 1) is fundamental and should be an old story by this time.

3. *He must play his position so that he can make an adequate shot even though badly exposed through a mediocre return of service by his partner.*

Since a well-played return of service is difficult to make, the initial position of player **N** is based in part on the assumption that the return of service may be weak. If the return *is* weak, he will need time as well as anticipation. Anticipation has been covered. Player **N** gains a moment by locating himself just inside the service line, rather than close to the net where he could be volleyed at from point-blank range. His position near the line separating the service courts enables him to cover volleys struck by either the server or the net man.

By proper team play the receiving team can make many seemingly impossible saves of forceful shots made off poor returns of service. (One such save, by an alert modified net man, is illustrated in Figure 20.) Naturally, there are some returns of service that can make the modified net position untenable. Suppose, for example, that the receiver hits a short lob which the net man can obviously murder. The receiver should yell, "Back!" to warn his partner that a quick retreat is in order. Even then an alert modified net man can scram for the baseline, or toward open wide angles, and manage to save the day.

At times the modified net man is in a spot where he has to make incredibly fast decisions. (The "let-go-by" dilemma is illustrated in

This point shows team play at its best. It occurred during a professional match pitting Budge and Gonzales against Kramer and Segura.

Budge, **B,** served to Segura, **M,** who tried to slip a return down the middle. But alert net man Gonzales, **A,** moved over and volleyed crisp and low to the center near modified net man Kramer, **N.** In a split second the receiving team had to decide which player had the better chance to make an effective return. Kramer, **N,** could reverse direction and reach the ball, but he would have to make a very difficult volley. Moreover, Kramer had to know where Segura would be, and whether Segura would anticipate his decision. Finally—all in a split second—Kramer let the ball go by; and Segura, who had started for the net, reversed his field beautifully to cover Gonzales' volley. And noting that Gonzales was slow to return to his proper net position, Segura rifled a backhand drive down the line for a marvelous placement. Great tennis!

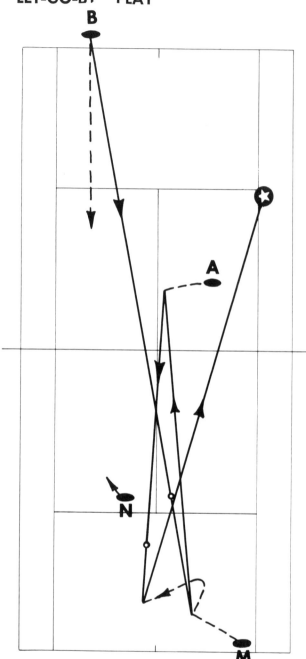

Figure 25

Figure 25.) Having a partner who can anticipate, take care of himself in the forecourt, and make "impossible" gets is, needless to say, a great comfort to the harassed receiver. It gives him the confidence to take chances, to try to keep the opponents off balance with occasional tricky shots (like slipping a return down the sideline or through the center) which he would otherwise be afraid to risk.

In the final analysis, the duel being presented here is not just receiver versus the server's service, but also receiver versus the server's first volley. If the server is presented with a "cinch" first volley, the point is usually as good as lost. To get factual data on the over-all pattern of this vitally important dual in doubles, the two 1954 semi-finals matches at Longwood, involving Australian and United States teams, were monitored. In the first Seixas and Trabert defeated Hartwig and Fraser, 8-6, 8-6, 5-7, 6-4; and in the second Hoad and Rosewall over-came Richardson and Talbert, 6-2, 6-4, 12-10.

Table XI shows the points won and lost by the receivers, how many strokes it took to decide the point, the types of first volleys used against the receivers, and the number of first volleys against each receiver resulting in won or lost points. The table makes a number of compelling points:

1. The receiver generally loses about one and one-half times as many points through errors as he wins outright with his return of service. However, before you accept this as a satisfactory par, note that Lew Hoad won eleven points outright while erring on only ten. An excellent performance!

2. The majority of points won by the receiving team are won on the return of service stroke itself, rather than on subsequent strokes in the rally (a total of 95 as against 76). In other words, the first volley is the most difficult volley for the server to make successfully, but once he has made it he has a good chance to win with it. This underlines the tremendous value of getting the return of service safely and effectively into play.

3. The receiving team generally loses twice as many points as it wins. This checks out with the average length of a game in doubles: six points, four won against two lost. Note that Hoad once again stands out as the best receiver of the afternoon. He won twenty-two points, while losing only thirty-one.

4. Provided the receiving team does not make an error in returning service, its chances of winning the point are almost equal to those of the serving team (171 won as against 206 lost, or 45 per cent of the time). The only team showing up poorly in this respect was Richardson

and Talbert, who took a beating from the deep, savage first volleys of Hoad and Rosewall.

5. If the receiving team does not win the point on the successful return of service, and the serving team does not win the point on its first volley, a rally ensues, which again favors the serving team, since it is first to gain the command of the net. The ratio of seventy-six wins to ninety-seven losses for the receiving team, or approximately 45 per cent, is the same as 4 above.

During these matches, when a particularly strong server, like Trabert, was going great guns and winning his game handily, the Aussies would suddenly switch tactics to try to upset him. This they did by deliberately taking long chances—they slugged the return of service down the line or cross-court at irretrievable angles, figuring that they had nothing to lose. If two desperation shots happened to go for placements, they were back in business with a good chance to break a hitherto impenetrable serve and gain a terrific psychological advantage.

In summary, it is well to re-emphasize the importance of the return of service and the high order of team play required if the receiving pair are to have a chance to break service. Probably it is their excellence in these particular aspects of play that has carried the Australians to doubles supremacy over all other nations. The 1950 U. S. Doubles Championship (data in Table IX) is a perfect case in point: Australian returns of service and court tactics made it possible for Bromwich and Sedgman to move into the offensive position at net 51 per cent of the time; while Talbert and Mulloy were able to do so only 18 per cent of the time! Young doubles players should seek to emulate Bromwich and Lott in this department. They were able to mix up the drive, dink, and lob returns with a deceptive similarity of motion guaranteed to keep the serving team off balance. They combined force with finesse, attack with defense; and when no openings existed, they used great resources to create them.

CHAPTER VI

Net Play

It is impossible to overemphasize the importance of net play in doubles. Tables IV and V show graphically that approximately 33 per cent of all strokes, and what is more important, 54 per cent of all winning shots in championship doubles, are made from the net position. Since only 26 per cent of the winning shots are made with ground strokes and lobs from the vicinity of the base line, the net position has about a two-to-one advantage over the base-line position. Excluding the service and return of service, which must be played from the base line, the advantage of the net position over the base line jumps to the staggering figure of four-to-one! This is borne out in Table VI, which shows the overwhelming potency of the overhead and volley compared with other strokes. Thus, taking the offensive position at the net at every opportunity is a "must," and should be practiced till it becomes second nature.

To play the net effectively, you must first learn:

1. *To anticipate.*

Play at the net is incredibly fast, particularly when all four players are in the forecourt banging away at one another. To give an idea of just how fast, Tilden's and Gonzales' serves were timed at 111 miles per hour, which makes the average flight of the ball faster than that of any other sport, including golf and baseball. A shot traveling at 111 miles per hour covers the whole length of a tennis court in 0.48 seconds, and in a hard-hitting exchange at net the players have about *0.20 seconds* to follow the flight of the ball, note the opponent's position,

95

make up their minds what to do, and stroke the ball! So to have a chance to make effective returns, the topflight player must anticipate with split-second timing and yet get a jump on the ball. The net man must not only anticipate the shots of his opponents (by studying their stroking techniques, footwork, and other factors that give away their intentions), but also he must know his partner so well that he can tell where the partner's next shot is going and what type of return it is likely to produce. Keen anticipation helped to make players like the Dohertys, Richards, Borotra, Allison, Brugnon, Seixas, and Lott so marvelous at doubles. It takes many hours of practice.

2. *To move to the best position.*

The net player must be in the proper position at the right moment. Since two men cannot cover completely the width of the net, particularly when the opponents are stroking the ball from a wide angle, or from close in, the net players must shift position in order to present, as a team, the best coverage of the court considering the position of the opponents and the type of stroke about to be made. This may require moving in close, to one side, crowding the center, drifting back, or waiting until the last second to draw the shot and then moving rapidly to cover an opening. As noted early and often, anticipation helps tremendously in ascertaining and moving to the ideal position. Also, you must keep an eye on your partner, know his habits, and have some prearranged understandings about certain types of shots, in order to cover the court width and prevent shots from being driven between teammates. Position shifts continually at the net with the changing position of the ball, so there is no tolerating laziness. A half-step can mean the difference between winning and losing a point.

Not incidentally, proper position play includes keeping out of your partner's way when he is stroking the ball. You may have to duck low so that he may hit an overhead or angled shot over you, or give ground to allow him more swinging room.

3. *To be alert.*

The exciting, rapid-fire play most characteristic of doubles comes at the net. To play topflight doubles the net player must keep his brain ticking and his reflexes sharp. It's not enough to get your racquet on the ball; you must think and then make the proper tactical return—all in a split second. Catlike quickness, excellent balance, and the racquet always in the best ready position make for the alert player. Again, practice is the answer.

Once anticipation, position, and alertness have been learned, two wonderful things will happen: you will have a lot more fun because you will get more balls back, have longer and more exciting rallies; you will improve your game by about fifteen points and begin to win more matches.

The strokes at the disposal of the net player are numerous and varied. They include the deep volley, angle volley, drop volley, half-volley, lob volley, deep overhead, and angled overhead. In addition, there are ground strokes: the dink shot, soft-angled topped drive, flat drive, and lob. As shown in Table VIII, the most productive of winners is the deep volley, responsible for 30 per cent of all winning strokes in doubles. Next in frequency are the deep overhead and the angle volley, which account for 11 and 9 per cent of all winners. It is interesting to note from this same table that the ranking order of the various strokes is altered when one considers lethality, or the per cent of winners which are outright placements. In lethality the angled overhead is well out in front with 89 per cent of all placement winners. Following are the angle volley, deep overhead, and deep volley with 60 per cent, 45 per cent, and 26 per cent lethality. This important piece of information indicates that once the opponents are drawn out of position or forced to hit up a weak shot, the alert net player takes advantage by pounding an angle shot to the open country for a clean placement. Clearly it is profitable to have in your repertoire an assortment of sharply angled strokes. To put it another way, many net strokes are used largely as tactical weapons to force the opponents to volley up or to lose position so that the haymaker can be applied.

Before proceeding with types of point-winning plays at the net, let us dwell for a bit on proper position at the net—considered, as always, from the steam standpoint.

Figures 26 and 27 show the best basic position for net play—that is, the best position against the majority of opposing positions and strokes. Barring special emergencies, this is the position to strive for, and generally it should be returned to after each stroke much as one returns to the center of the base line in singles after each stroke. The players are approximately eight feet from the net and sixteen feet apart. The exact distance from the net should be determined by the height and speed of reaction of the players. Note well that the players should crowd the center of the court: here the combined reaches of the net men, insufficient to complete coverage of the net, are concentrated on covering the low portion of the net over which

This diagram is an important one to remember—it shows the best basic position for the net team, players **A** and **B.** Note that they are as close to the net—about eight feet—as is consistent with their ability to protect against a lob. Also they are packing the center: each has eight feet to cover in the middle and ten feet on the alley side.

To emphasize the advantages of this basic position for offensive volleying, opposing team **M** and **N** is shown in the deep volleying formation used *circa* 1900. Note that players **A** and **B** can easily volley at the feet of players **M** and **N** to draw errors or weak returns. Also they have plenty of room to angle volley past the opposition for placements at aim points 1 and 2.

Like the *en garde* position in fencing, the basic net formation is the soundest of all operating positions: the team should start from it and return to it whenever possible throughout the progress of the point. To see how it works defensively turn to Figure 27.

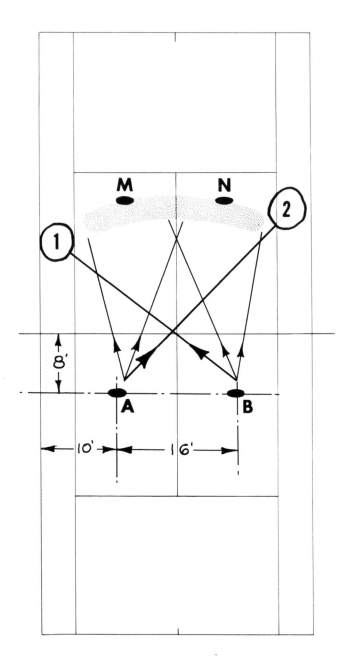

Figure 26

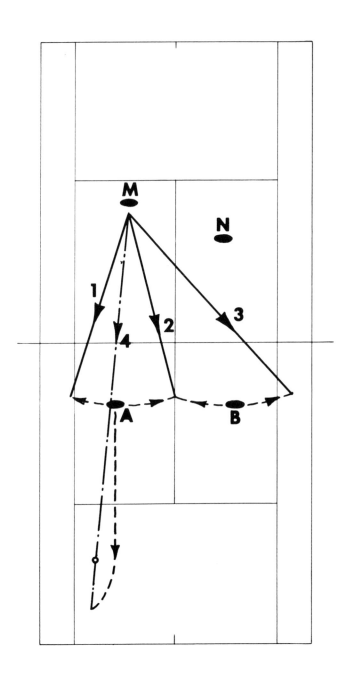

Figure 27

The net position shown in Figure 26 is basic for defensive as well as offensive play.

Most volleys in doubles are hit deep down the middle. Such volleys, represented by number 2 in the diagram, can be hit with great severity because they have the full length of the court to travel. Obviously the net men must be able to cover these shots quickly, before they are driven past them. So net players **A** and **B** pack the center to present the best defense against the normal offense.

Players **A** and **B** are able to cover down-the-line or angle volleys, depicted as shots 1 and 3, even though they are packing the center. Here's why: down-the-line volleys usually must be hit up a bit, and hence somewhat softly, because of the higher level of the net at the sidelines; and the angle volleys have just a short distance to travel, so if they are hit hard they are likely to sail out of court. The softness of the shot gives net players **A** and **B** a little added time to move to the sidelines.

The basic net position is close enough to the net so that few volleys will land at the vulnerable area at the player's feet. And alert net player **A** still has time to get back to cover lob volley 4.

most shots will come. This pack-the-center strategy is used by the Australians, and it counts heavily for their success in volleying exchanges. The exact distance apart of the players is determined by their reach and the speed of their anticipation and reflex action.

The positions in Figure 26 should be memorized. It will be referred to from time to time as the "basic net position."

A number of circumstances force a modification of the basic net position. These are:

1. If the opponents are about to lob, the net team should drop back a step or so at the proper moment to prepare for an overhead smash.

2. If the opponents are forced to hit up a weak shot, the net team should move closer to volley down or angle volley for a placement.

3. If the opposing players are also at net, it is wise to move in a bit closer to the net and crowd the center of the court. This increases the chances of volleying down at the feet of the opponents without jeopardizing the defense.

4. During rapid net exchanges a team or a player may often anticipate, from the shot he or his partner makes and the position of the opponent about to strike the ball, the exact area of the return. Immediately one or both men can move to cover that area and volley away a kill. This can be done safely, even though it means deserting the basic net position.

5. When the opponents are about to play a ball from a wide angle, the net team must shift position in order to present the best defense. Such a situation is illustrated in Figures 28 and 29. Obviously, the net team should not just turn in its tracks as in Figure 28, but must shift position as in Figure 29 in order best to cover the wide angles of return. The net team should practice shifting one man forward toward the center and the other back toward the sideline—the proper distance for each shift depending on the angle from which the return is about to be made. Remember, the wider the angle the better chance the opponents have to slip by a passing shot.

6. If one partner at the net is forced out of position, the other partner must shift his position to cover for him. For example, if your partner is drawn in close to the net to volley, you should fall back a step to be prepared to cover a lob over his head.

7. As noted in Chapter V, serves to various parts of the service court require the net man and inrushing server to alter position to cover the court to best advantage.

8. If the opponents are about to drive from the base line, the net

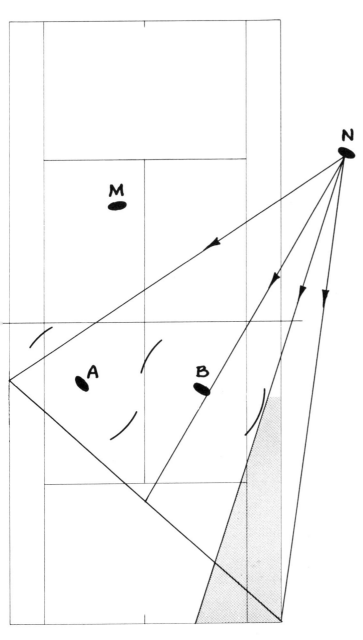

There are times when the basic net position does not present the best defensive net position. Here is a case where player **N** has been forced off court by an angled shot and is set to hit a ground-stroke return. Players **A** and **B** have maintained their basic net position and merely turned in place to face player **N**. It is clear that they present an overlapping defense in the center (parentheses represent reach), while leaving the entire shaded area open for an easy placement by player **N**.

Figure 28

The correct defensive net position is shown here, in contrast with Figure 28, against returns from wide angles. Player **A** has moved forward to his right two steps to cover sharp cross-court returns, and player **B** has dropped back to his right to cover down-the-line shots. Between them (parentheses show reach) they blanket the court. To prevent misunderstandings the partners should call for any lobs set up by player **N**.

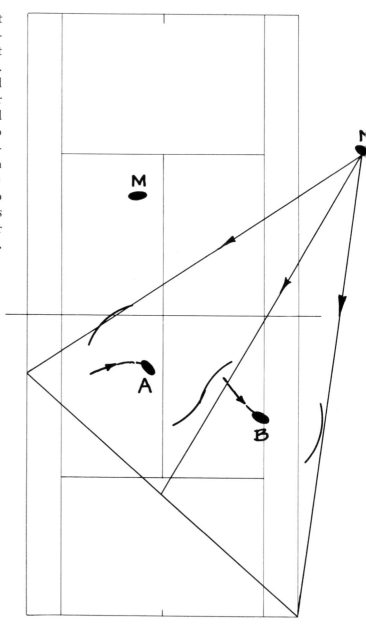

Figure 29

team should crowd the net to volley down and angle volley more strongly.

Important in proper net position is a complete understanding between partners. Only practice can develop such an understanding and the confidence that it brings. Nothing makes a team feel more stupid than an Alphonse and Gaston act, when both partners are within reach of the ball but then let it sail serenely between them for a placement. Here are six general rules that should be followed to prevent embarrassment:

1. If a ball is hit straight down center, it should usually be taken by the player with his forehand toward the center. With two right-handed players this means the man in the backhand court.

2. If a ball is hit cross-court in between the net players, it should be taken by the man on the opposite side of the court from which the shot is made. Thus, a shot hit cross-court from the opponent's forehand court should be taken by the net player on the forehand side; and a shot hit crosscourt from the opponent's backhand court should be played by the net man on the backhand side. The reasoning behind these assignments is fairly obvious. Suppose, for example, that all four players are at net and the opponent in the forehand court plays a cross-court volley. The net man facing him in the backhand court would have a hard time stroking the ball as it passed by him at a wide angle; but the net man in the forehand court would be faced directly toward the path of the ball, and thus be able to meet it squarely and stroke it much more easily.

3. For a rapid exchange at point-blank range at the net, it is often best for the man who last hit the ball to take shots returned down the center. It is usually easier for the hitter to follow the ball and anticipate the return.

4. Lobs hit down the middle should be smashed by the man in the backhand court, since his forehand is toward the center of the court. Otherwise, lobs should be taken by the player to whose side the lob is hit.

5. When in doubt, the partners must yell, "Yours," or, "Mine." Often a net player may be caught on the wrong foot or off balance by the surprise tactics of the opponents, and he must alert his partner to take the ball. Form the habit of yelling signals—and make them loud.

6. On a return of service hit down the center the net man usually moves over to try to volley it away. However, the server must be prepared to back him up, for often at the last second the net man will find he cannot reach the ball or cannot play it effectively and

must let it go by. When there is an emergency, the net man should duck out of the way to give his partner a better chance to volley.

Up to this point we have been laying the groundwork and setting forth the fundamentals for good doubles play. With all the mechanics firmly in mind, you are ready to take up the most interesting and exciting part of doubles: the actual tactics of net play.

Net play starts—logically enough—with the initial volley of the serving team. This volley is usually made by the server since, as we have already noted, 85 per cent of returns of service are hit cross-court at him as he moves in to the net.

The server must realize that his first volley is the most difficult one for him to make. It is also his most important volley. Study of Table XI has shown that over half of the points won by the serving team after successful returns of service are won on the first volley. Many other points are won because a strong first volley has set the stage. On the other hand, the table shows that the server wins only 15 per cent more points outright on the first volley than he loses because of errors. In fact, after a successful return of service, the serving team must really stick to its guns, for its chances of winning drop from two-to-one to only 1.2-to-one over the receiving team.

All too often the server merely keeps the ball in play rather than concentrating on placing this important volley carefully. To make the most effective first volley the server should follow his serve in close to the net (from nine to fifteen feet), as recommended in Chapter IV. He should also bend at the knees and get well down to the ball. It will prevent many costly errors.

There are essentially two defensive formations that may greet the server as he starts to make his volley. They are illustrated in Figure 30, and depend on whether the receiver followed in his return of service or remained in the back court. The proper aim points for the first volley in each case are shown.

To maintain the most favorable offensive position the server, **B,** must volley safely as deep, as low, and as near the center of the court as possible. This means that the server should volley either at the feet of the receiver, **M,** as he moves in toward the net position to force him to volley or half-volley up, or deep to the base line if the receiver remains in the back court. Remember that the receiver is the last man to make his move toward the net, so it is obviously easier to put the ball at his feet. At the same time the server, in volleying near the center of the court, should be careful to keep his volley away from the opposing net man, **N,** so that he cannot intercept the shot.

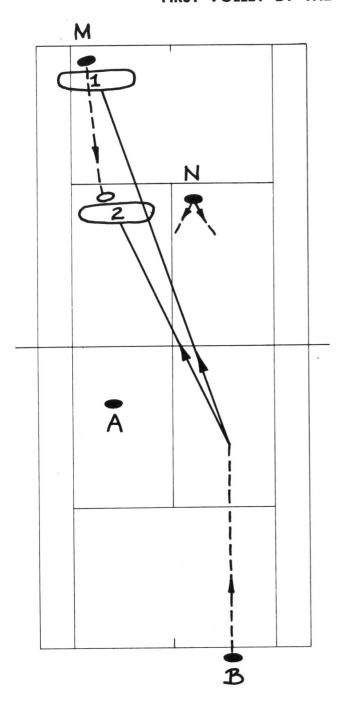

Figure 30

Receiver **M** will either remain on the base line or follow his return of service in to the net. If **M** remains in the back court, server **B** should generally volley the return as deep and near the center as possible to aim point 1. If **M** moves in to the net, server **B** should generally volley at the receiver's feet as near the center as possible to aim point 2.

These general aim points are used by the server in the majority of cases, but not when he is presented with a weak return that may more effectively be volleyed for a placement, as in Figures 34, 36, 37, 38, 39, and 50.

The wisdom of the deepest and lowest volley to the center shows immediately when the next sequence of shots is considered. The angle of return open to the receiver, whether he is volleying or half-volleying from near the center of the forecourt or playing a ground stroke from the middle of the base line, is limited. And the offensive team is often able to take advantage of the central position of the defensive team by crowding the net and volleying the return away at a sharp angle for a placement. These situations, and the proper aim points for them, are illustrated in Figures 31 and 32. Note that the server must continue to move in toward the net after making his first volley to attain the best offensive net position. The only exception: when the opponents are about to lob, in which case the server should judge his move according to the depth of the lob.

If the server's first volley is shallow and wide instead of deep down the center, he puts his team in trouble. Figure 33 shows how the serving team stands to lose its offensive advantage: receiver **M** has a better opportunity to make an offensive return, and the receiving team is in a better position to defend against the next return by the serving team.

If the advancing server is handed a weak, high return of service, or if he finds the receiving team out of position, the server need not adhere to the general rule of making his first volley deep to the center. Instead, he simply hits away his first volley for a placement—as shown in Figures 34 through 39.

A sound principle already mentioned in Chapter IV and emphasized in Figures 34 through 39 is that the twist serve should be followed well in to the net in order to volley down from an offensive position. Unless the volleyer is within about six to nine feet of the net, he is not in position to take advantage of many opportunities to volley away placements by hitting either at sharp angles or down on the ball at terrific speed. (Quist was a master at following his serve well in to the net so that he could make such offensive volleys.) If the server is too far back, he is usually forced to volley up, which necessarily takes the sting out of the shot and often provides a setup for the opposition to move in on and kill (see Figure 35).

Consider next how the server should play his first volley when the receiver makes a return of service which is difficult to handle. The two returns of service which give most trouble are the dink shot and the topped cross-court drive. A number of typical problems are depicted in Figures 40 through 43. In each case the server must use his head as well as his playing skill to save the point.

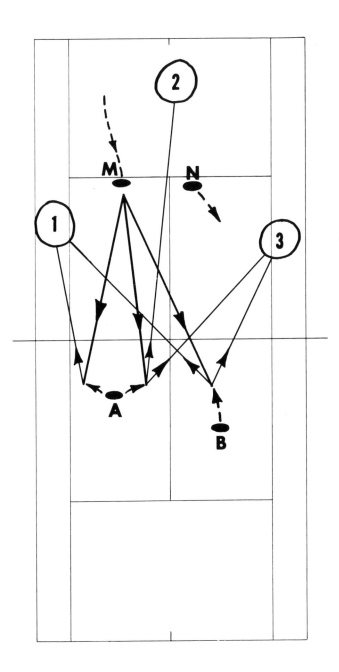

This diagram shows the advantage gained by server **B** when he carries out the suggestion illustrated in Figure 30—placing his first volley close to the middle of the court at the feet of advancing receiver **M**. Receiver **M** has to volley or half-volley up cross-court, to the middle or down the line as shown. Now, as server **B** continues to move in, he and his partner can win the point with angle volleys to aim points 1 or 3, or a deep volley down the middle to aim point 2 if player **M** or **N** moves too quickly to cover the wide-angle area.

Figure 31

If receiver **M** fails to follow his return of service in to net, and server **B** has placed his first volley deep to the middle as recommended in Figure 30, the serving team is in this excellent position.

As receiver **M** starts to play a ground stroke from near the base line, players **A** and **B** can afford to move in to crowd the net. In this way server **B** has opened up easy opportunities for his team to angle volley for the point to aim points 1 and 3. Also net man **A** can volley away to the familiar open diagonal at aim point 2.

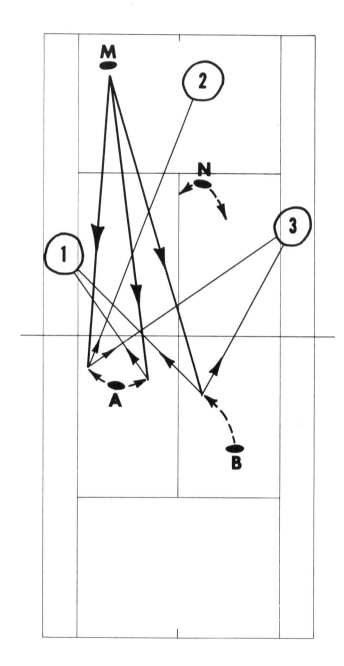

Figure 32

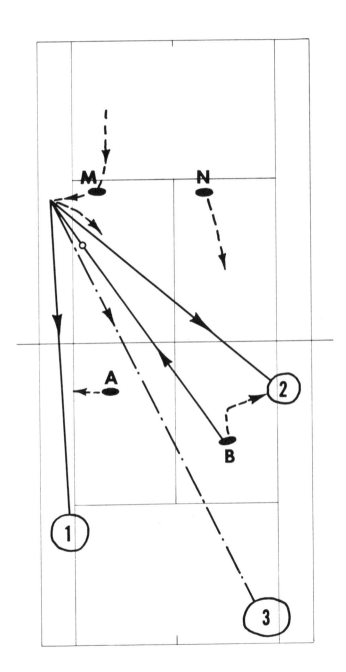

In contrast with Figures 31 and 32, here is a weak first volley by server **B**. The consequences of a wide, shallow first volley can be disastrous to the serving team. Note that as receiver **M** follows in behind his return he has plenty of time to swerve to his right to play a ground stroke. Receiver **M** has a great opportunity to take the offensive away from the serving team by threading a shot down the line to aim point 1, hitting a topped drive or dink to the middle or cross-court to aim point 2, or lobbing to aim point 3 at the farthest corner of the court. Then the receiving team, **M** and **N**, can move well in to net to take advantage of the weak return expected from the serving team.

Figure 33

Here is an ideal situation for server **B.** He has served an American twist, as recommended, deep to the backhand corner and pulled receiver **M** to the middle. When receiver **M** hits a weak, high backhand return, server **B** runs well in to the net so that he can angle volley down crisply into the open area for an easy placement. Or he can just as easily bang his volley down the line for the placement.

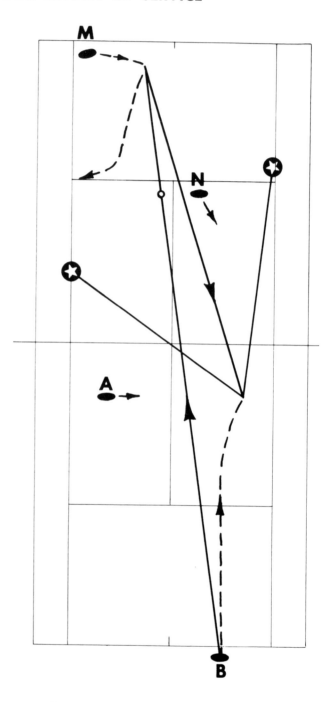

Figure 34

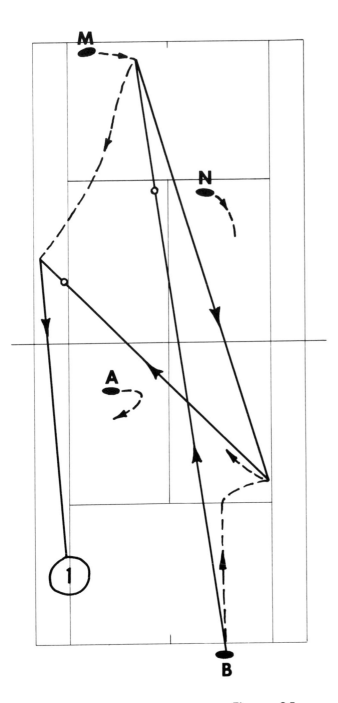

This point begins exactly as the point in Figure 34. The deep twist serve draws receiver **M** to the middle and he makes the same weak, high backhand return of service. But server **B** is slow in moving in—and what a difference it makes! Instead of volleying down with pace on the ball for a placement, he now has to volley up, without any sting in the shot, from near the service line. As a result he cannot volley safely down the line or near the center. So he volleys cross-court and hands receiver **M** a good chance to turn the tide in his favor with a drive to a spot like aim point 1.

After working hard to develop a setup, do not flub it by being lazy in your run for the net.

Figure 35

Here is another easy point for the server, who gets up to the net in a hurry on a weak, high backhand return of service. It really does not matter to him whether he has a forehand or backhand volley: he can drive either forehand or backhand past modified net man **N** for a placement as depicted. Also he can angle volley from the backhand side for the point if receiver **M** comes up the middle.

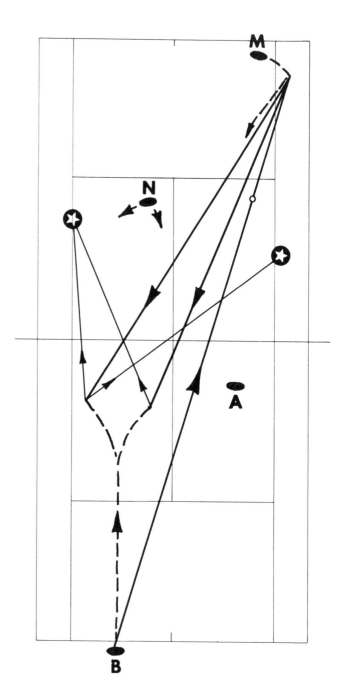

Figure 36

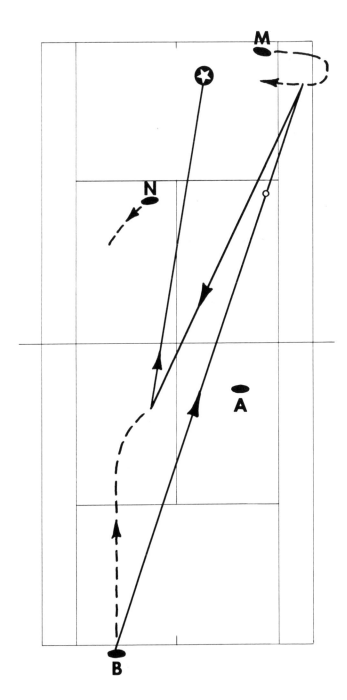

The point illustrated here differs from that in Figure 36 in a few important details—details the server must note carefully if he is to take maximum advantage of the momentary openings.

The receiving team has made two mistakes, which allow server **B** to turn his first volley into a placement. First, receiver **M** has run around a serve to the backhand corner in order to hit a forehand return of service. This immediately opens up the possibility of a first volley to the middle because receiver **M** will obviously have a difficult time scrambling back fast enough to cover the center. Second, modified net man **N** has started to move to his right to cover a possible angle volley just a bit too soon. As soon as server **B** adds this bit of information to what he has already noted, he quickly elects to volley deep down the center. And he is rewarded with a lovely placement.

Figure 37

As in Figure 37, the server has in this point taken advantage of poor position play by the receiving team.

First, receiver **M** has "rolled" in anticipation of an American twist service, and run around it to play a forehand return of service. This left the whole right side of the receiving team court open unless player **M** scrambled back quickly. As server **B** came in to net he noted that receiver **M** was slow in getting into position and was not following his return into the net. So he dumped a little drop volley at an angle out of reach of modified net man **N** for a fine placement.

Note the alert play of net man **A**. He moved toward the center because of the bounce point of the serve. Then, on seeing the drop volley, he moved back and to his left to cover a down-the-line or lob return if the stop volley is too deep.

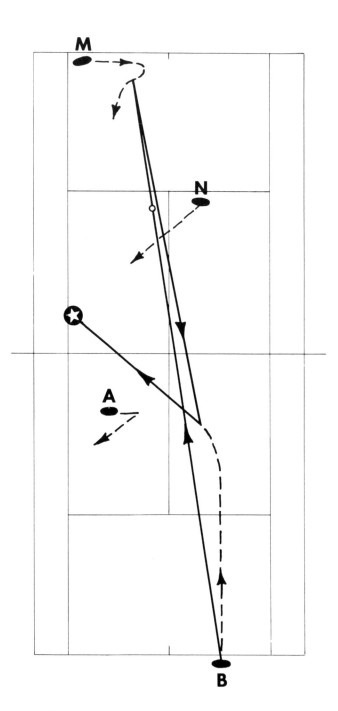

Figure 38

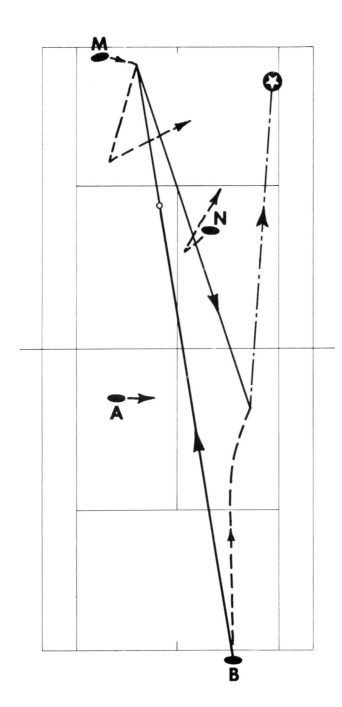

The first volley is a gem—the kind of thing that makes tennis galleries swoon. It was made in the U. S. Nationals by none other than Harry Hopman, the Australian Davis Cup Captain.

The return of service by receiver **M** looked very good to his partner, modified net man **N**. In fact player **N** figured it would force server **B** to volley up rather weakly cross-court. So he waited until what he thought was the proper moment and then started to poach in order to intercept the volley. But server **B**, Hopman, was too clever. Despite the fact that he was facing a difficult first volley from close to the ground, he was calmly surveying the situation. Just as he was getting set to make the standard return, a cross-court volley, he detected player **N** start his poach too soon, and this gave him the opening he needed. With split-second reflexes, server **B** switched tactics and lofted a beautiful lob volley just out of reach of player **N** down the line for a placement. Lott, Parker, and Rosewall make this difficult shot look ridiculously simple.

Figure 39

Receiver **M** has hit a well-placed dink shot that forces server **B** to volley up from near the net. This means the server cannot volley down the line effectively because he is under the high part of the net. Also he cannot volley anywhere within reach of modified net man **N**, who is advancing toward the net for a possible kill. Therefore, the server is compelled to dump a short cross-court volley to aim point 1, or, if receiver **M** is slow coming up, a deeper cross-court volley wide to aim point 2. Receiver **M** can cover either shot easily so that the serving team must set its defenses quickly to meet the return.

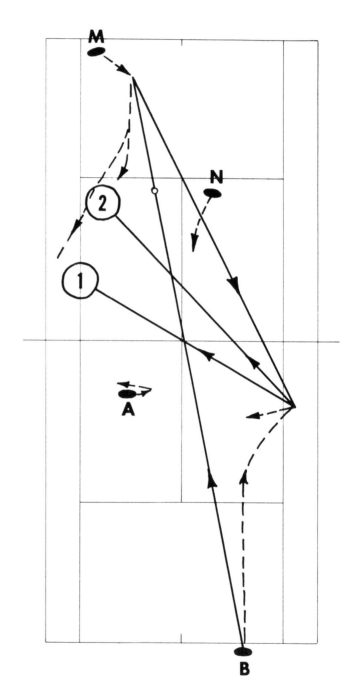

Figure 40

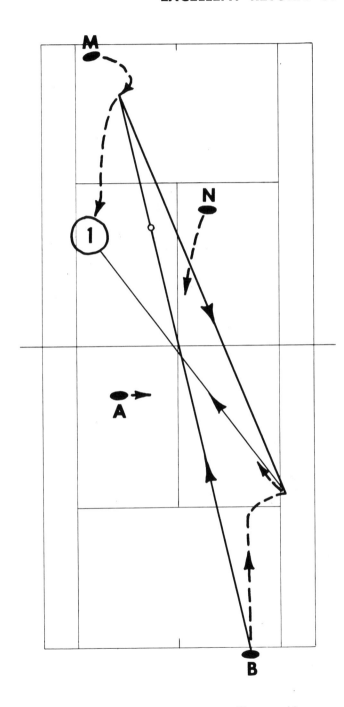

A fairly shallow serve has given receiver **M** an opportunity to move up and run around the ball. He pounds a topped drive deep to the corner of the service court. Server **B** has to swerve sharply to his right and either volley or half-volley up defensively. Under these circumstances server **B** is content just to get the ball back safely. Any shot down the line is too risky: all he can do is to try to play the ball cross-court wide past player **N** to aim point 1, and then move into a defensive volleying position.

Figure 41

Here is a valuable lesson for the server to learn. Receiver **N** has placed a fine low return of service down the middle. Net man **A** has moved over for the ball, but at the last instant he decides that lunging for a low backhand volley might set one up for the opposing modified net man **N** (toward whom the ball would most likely be hit), or result in an error. The server, aware of this possibility, backs up his partner and swings through on the shot. He saves the point, at least temporarily, by hitting a difficult shot safely past his ducking partner wide of player **N**; otherwise the return of service would have slipped through for a placement.

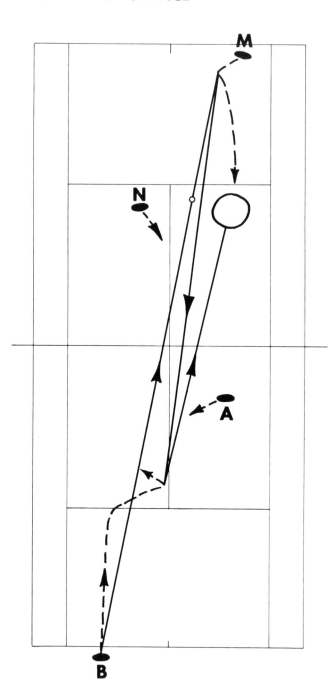

Figure 42

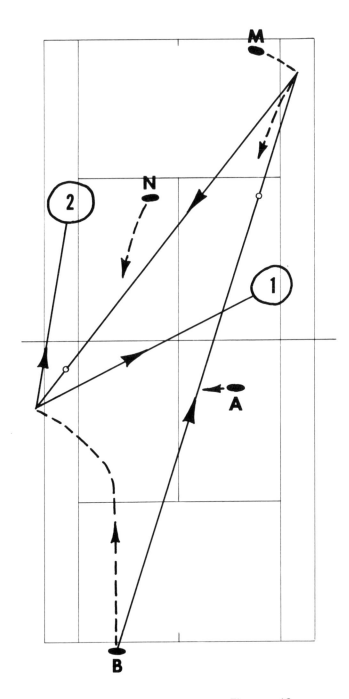

Receiver **M** has made a near-perfect dink shot. His partner **N** is moving in to kill a volley that must be made from so close to the net that it would have to be dug out of the turf. Rather than volley up to the inrushing opponents from an awkward spot, the server has wisely decided to slow down and let the return bounce. This gives more of a chance to make the conventional cross-court shot to aim point 1 or, if the bounce is high enough, to slip a backhand drive down the line to aim point 2.

Figure 43

To analyze the effectiveness of the various types of first volleys played by the server, data were taken on seven sets of championship play (presented in Table XIII). The data confirm beautifully the general rule to hit the first volley deep, and they show that the server can win a very high percentage of weak returns by playing the wide angle or down-the-line first volley from close to the net. No one—club player or internationalist—can afford to miss.

TABLE XIII

EFFECT OF TYPES OF SERVER'S FIRST VOLLEY
ON ULTIMATE OUTCOME OF POINT

Receiver Stays Back on Return

Types of Volleys

Deep		Semi-deep		Angled		Shallow		Down line		Hit up		Overhead	
Won	Lost	Won	Lost	Won	Lost	Won	Lost	Won	Lost	Won	Lost	Won	Lost
100	34	38	30	20	4	13	6	54	8	7	32	6	0

Receiver Follows Return In

Types of Volleys

Deep		At feet		Angled		Shallow		Hit up	
Won	Lost	Won	Lost	Won	Lost	Won	Lost	Won	Lost
23	10	17	3	5	2	26	15	3	10

Finally, the net man also has duties to perform as his partner advances after serving to make the first volley. He should always turn to see what his partner is doing. After all, his partner might have fallen down, dropped his racquet, got his signals mixed, or stopped to ogle a shapely redhead on the sidelines. Such emergencies require drastic action on the part of the net man.

If everything is in order and the server is in position to stroke the ball, the net man must note the type and direction of volley being made. Then he must rapidly sweep the opponents' court, determine the position of the modified net man and the receiver, and get into the best position for the opponents' next shot. Unless the net man follows this routine on each point, he may be caught out of position—especially by the modified net man who may be poaching to slam a weak first volley directly through his mid-section. On the other hand an alert net man can save many a poor first volley situation by anticipating the action of the opponents and being ready for the return at exactly the proper spot (see Figures 60 and 98).

The Plays at the Net

It is now time to move into complete plays at the net. This part of the game of doubles requires the utmost in tennis courtsmanship, finesse, patience, deception, and stroke production. It is a game of angles and position which calls for splitting the opposition wide open with angle shots and volleying through them down the middle for the point, or piling them up in the middle and then angling off a volley for the placement. Subtle play, not brute force, wins the net exchanges when all four players are in the forecourt. In general, the team that can play a step nearer the net has the advantage; they should be able to force the opposition to volley up.

It takes careful study to develop any real grasp of net play; and to be understandable diagrams of plays must be presented in some kind of sensible sequence. We have arranged the offensive (serving team) and defensive (receiving team) plays in the following sequence:

> The Deep Volley
> The Angle Volley
> Overhead Play
> The Soft and the Drop Volley
> The Lob Volley
> The Ground Strokes
> The Poach
> The Drift
> The Draw Play

The diagrams all illustrate authentic plays from tournament matches. In general, the plays are simple (so the diagrams do not have to be cluttered with lines indicating multiple exchanges), but they show clearly the basic methods of obtaining the opening.

Wherever possible the diagrams are presented in duplicate. The first figure shows the proper play for the offensive team, and the second figure reveals the proper counteraction for the defensive team.

The Deep Volley

The crisp, deep volley is a most important stroke in doubles —by almost two to one over any other stroke from the standpoint of producing winners.

There are logical reasons behind the fact—reasons involving the geometry of the court as well as tactics. All four players try to keep their volleys low, to avoid handing the opposition an advantage. On most shots they also try to generate sufficient pace to drive the ball through the opponents for a placement or to draw an error or force a weak return. Since the net is six inches lower in the middle, and since the court is about half again as long as it is wide as viewed by the volleyer, it is obvious that the volleyer has a much smaller chance of error on a low, fast volley hit deep down the middle. Another factor that causes the deep volley to produce so many winners: the favorite tactic of most doubles teams is to force the defense to spread by hitting one or more soft-angle volleys, and then banging a deep one through the opening in the middle. The old adage of divide and conquer applies to doubles, too.

Representative plays involving the offensive and defensive aspects of deep volley play are shown in Figures 44 through 55.

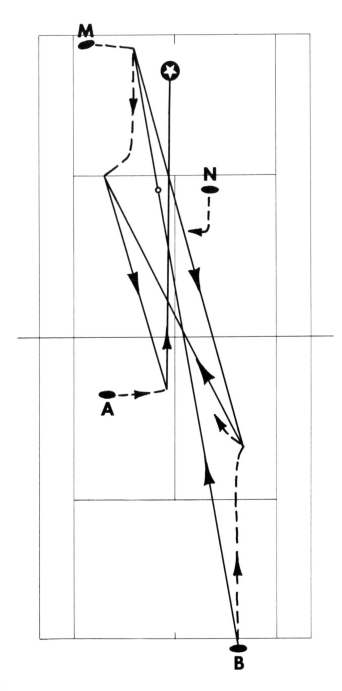

Figure 44

Receiver **M** is a bit slow in following in behind his return of service. Thus the first volley by server **B** forces **M** to volley up from his feet near the service line. Net man **A**, sensing a kill, moves over to intercept the return and boom a deep volley between the defenders for an easy placement.

This play begins as the point shown in Figure 44. However, this time receiver M really roars in to the net behind his return. Now he is able to return server B's first volley from waist height with a crisp, neatly placed volley to the middle for a placement.

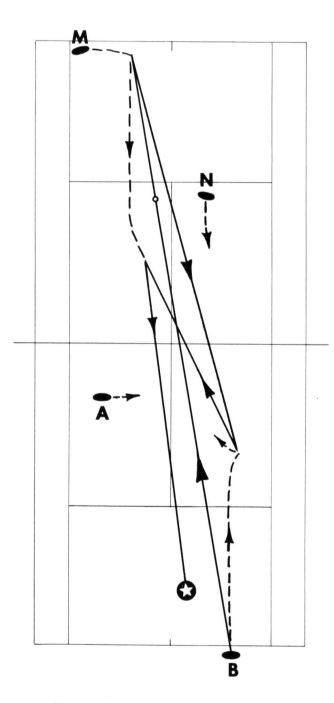

Figure 45

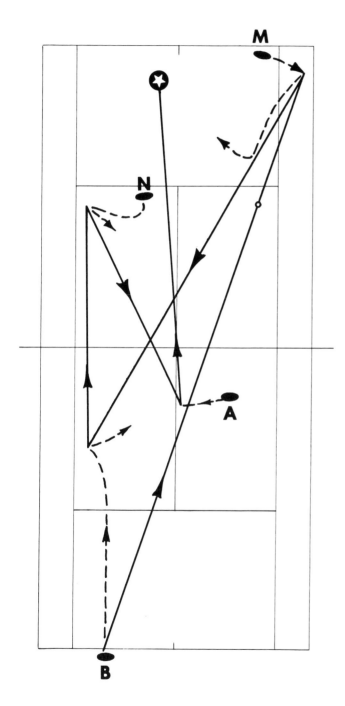

The key man in this play is modified net man **N.** Server **B's** first volley down the line catches him off guard. While he is able to reach the ball, he barely manages to return a weak volley to the center. Net man **A** scores easily with a deep backhand volley through the wide-open defense.

Figure 46

This time the first volley of server **B** is beautifully anticipated by modified net man **N.** He moves in unerringly, catches the volley at a higher point in its trajectory, and is able to volley down crisply through the middle to win a fine point.

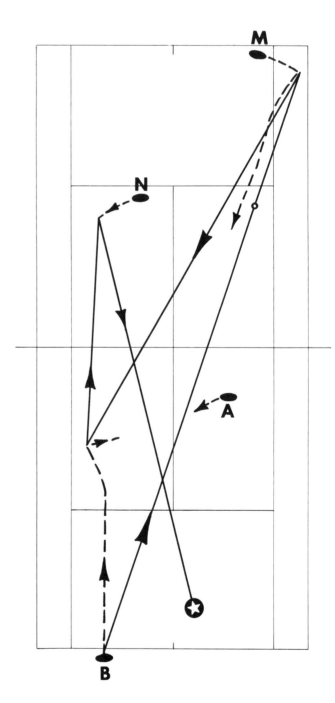

Figure 47

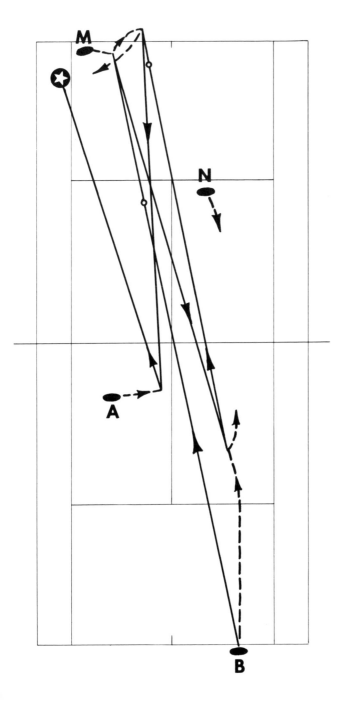

The key play in this diagram is the first volley by server **B**. He slips it just past modified net man **N**, deep to the middle. Receiver **M** has elected to remain in the back court and he is forced into making a defensive backhand return from beyond the base line. Net player **A** has taken advantage by inching toward the middle to cut off the return with a powerful deep volley for the point.

Figure 48

Here the roof falls in on the server because his first volley was shallow. Receiver **M** has time to recover, move in, and hit an offensive return. He chooses to hit a soft dink to the middle, thus drawing the serving team to the center. Then receiver **M** continues rapidly in to net to capitalize on his break. When server **B** volleys up, receiver **M** is near enough to the net to hit a severe volley down the line past scrambling net man **A** for his point.

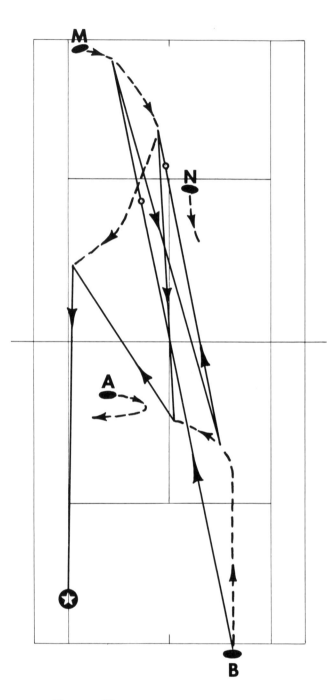

Figure 49

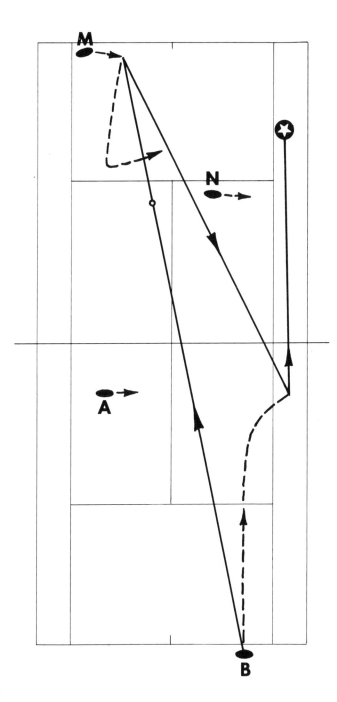

The key shot in this sequence is the dink return of service. Here the dink, which is a delicate shot, floats just a bare foot too high. This gives server **B**, who has sprinted rapidly in to the net, a chance to volley deep down the alley for the point. If he had been a bit slower, or if the shot had not floated, things would have been different (see Figure 51). A setup like this should be hit firmly by the server, but not too spectacularly, lest he end up with an error.

Figure 50

Just as in Figure 50 we have here a dink return of service. But this time it was perfect and did not float, so server **B** had to volley up. In case 1, modified net man **N** cleverly faked to cover the alley and cause server **B** to volley cross-court. Then he poached to his right and was presented with a ridiculously easy chance to volley deep for the point. It is up to receiver **M** to follow his dink in to net rapidly, so that he can volley away severely any return hit cross-court as in case 2. Such rare and perfect returns are often wasted by a receiver's mental or physical laziness.

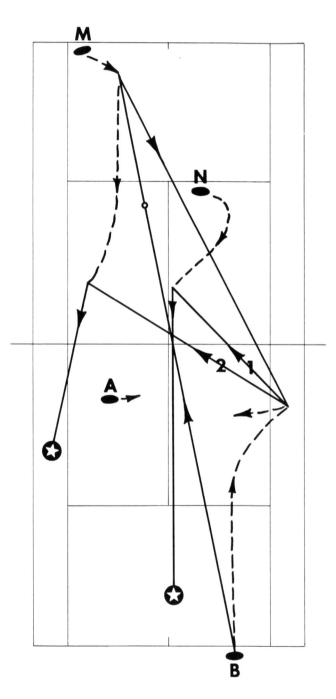

Figure 51

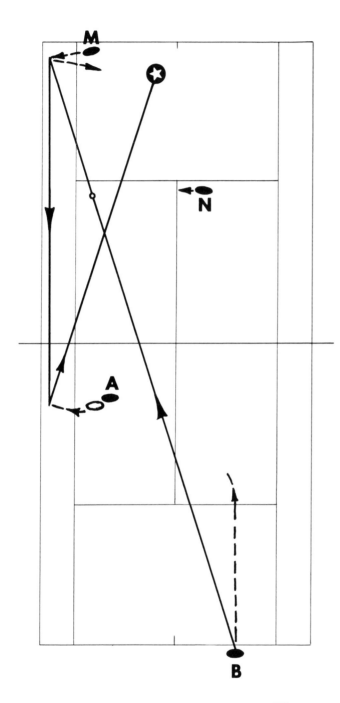

Figure 52

The net man is the important player in this point. On a serve to the forehand corner he has correctly moved toward the alley and back a step in order to cover a possible down-the-line return. When he is in fact presented with such a return, he has to move only a short distance and volley the ball deep to the open diagonal for the point. This shot is easy if the return of service is a bit high, and rather delicate if the return dips below the level of the net.

This is the same point as shown in Figure 52, but the net man has failed to position himself for the down-the-line return. So he has to dive for the ball, and fails in his attempt to hit the open diagonal. This gives modified net man **N** his chance to move over and hit a hard volley straight toward the base line for the point.

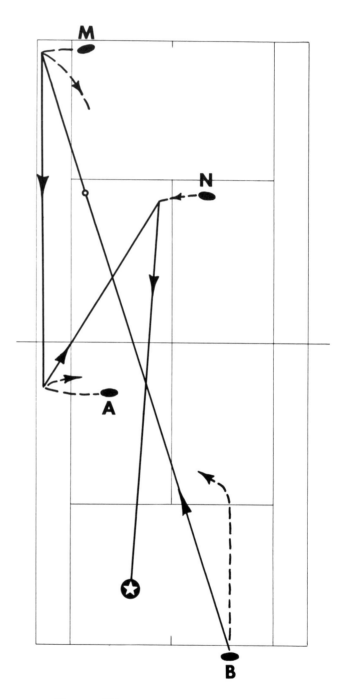

Figure 53

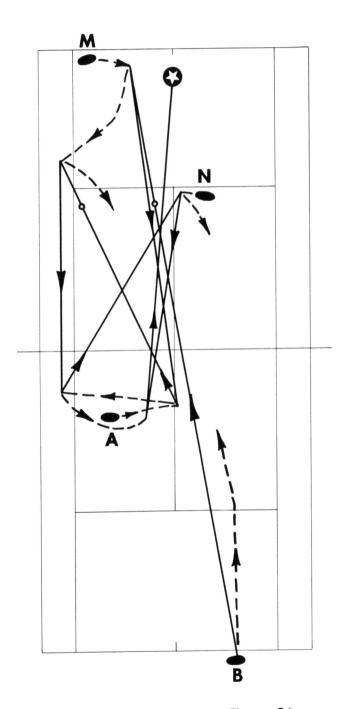

Figure 54

This is a superb exposition of net play in the National Doubles. The defense really had net man **A** on the run, but by agility and quick thinking he was able to win the point. He first crossed over to angle volley the return of service. Receiver **M** came in and, spotting the open alley, played a ground stroke down the line. But **A** anticipated and scrambled back to volley to the middle. Net man **N** covered the shot and again the defense sought to take advantage of a hole left by **A**. But net man **A** (Talbert, having one of his better days) rushed back and, noting **N** was moving toward the sideline to cover an angle volley, hit a beautiful deep volley behind him for the placement. Only lightning-fast reactions saved this point.

Here is a perfect example of the tactic of splitting the opposition wide open, then banging away down the middle for the point. Note the beautiful teamwork involved. Server **B** volleyed the dink return of service cross-court, and receiver **M** (Bromwich), following in behind his return, hit another dink shot cross-court. Server **B**, hoping to cross up **M** as he moved to the center, hit another cross-court angled volley. But **M** rushed to the sideline and hit still another sharply angled dink shot, which pulled **B** right off the court. **B** then tried to slip a shot down the alley, but net man **N** anticipated and covered the alley. Sensing that **A** would be moving to cover the center, he angled off his volley sharply cross-court. Net man **A** quickly reversed his field and tore back to hit a backhand ground stroke to the unprotected center. But cagey old Bromwich, **M**, moved over rapidly and, having successfully maneuvered the defense wide open, hit a deep volley through the center for a placement.

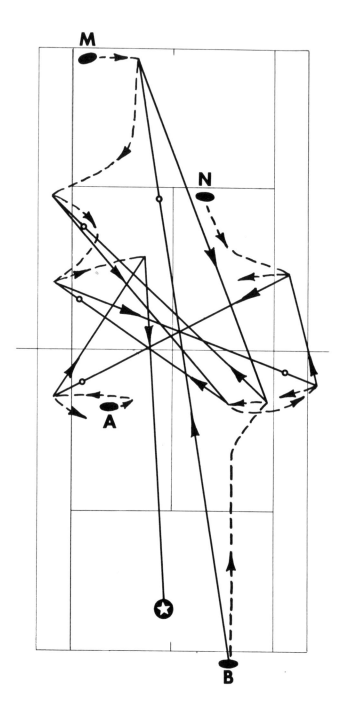

Figure 55

The Angle Volley

The angle volley is a potent, double-duty stroke. Used discriminately, it is an excellent put-away shot, and it is a weapon subtle beyond compare for drawing the opponents out of position to set up the kill.

Table VIII shows the angle volley has a lethality second only to the overhead. This should come as no great surprise, for in order to make a sharply angled volley, the striker must be close to the net and thus is often able to volley down with real pace on the ball. Then too, the angle volley is usually hit away from the opponents, whom you have maneuvered into covering the center of the court, toward a wide-open area. The sharp-angle volleys of top volley artists like Joe Hunt, Vincent Richards, Wilmer Allison, and Ted Schroeder were beautiful to behold, and through perfect timing and touch consistently hit the side stripes. The margin of error on an angle volley is practically nil: a ball hit inches too high or a bit too hard sails out; and one hit an inch too low, or with insufficient speed, is in the net. The overhead smash may be the overpoweringly explosive method of winning a point, but the angle volley is the neat, rapier-like, soul-satisfying way of turning the trick.

The use of the angle volley as a means of fencing for an opening is one of the basic tactics in doubles. It is true the deep volley wins more points than any other single stroke in doubles, but a major reason for its success is the angle volley which precedes it. These fencing shots are usually made off a rather low ball (one would go for a placement with a high ball). Thus, they often serve two purposes. First, they provide a means for getting out of a hole: instead of hitting up toward one of the opponents, which invites tragedy, a low, soft volley angled cross-court, a bit out of reach, may save the situation. (Do not forget the ball would pass over the lowest part of the net!) Second, the striker may at the same time split open the opponents' formation for a deep-volley winner on the next shot.

Sparring for an opening in doubles is much the same as in boxing. The game is at its best when all four players stand at the net, hitting away at one another to set up the opportunity for a knockout blow. And the real finesse, the quick thinking, anticipation, touch, and lightning-fast reflexes combine to make doubles one of the best of all sports.

Diagrams of actual championship plays involving the angle volley in both its roles follow in Figures 56 through 67. Other angle-volley diagrams may be found in the section on poaching in this chapter.

This is a classic angle volley. The stage is set perfectly by server **B.** First, he gets well in to net and volleys the return of service to the middle at the feet of advancing receiver **M.** Then he keeps moving in to the net to take advantage of the defensive return hit up by player **M.** From this vantage point, having forced the opposition to the center, server **B** can win with a routine volley to the wide-open spaces.

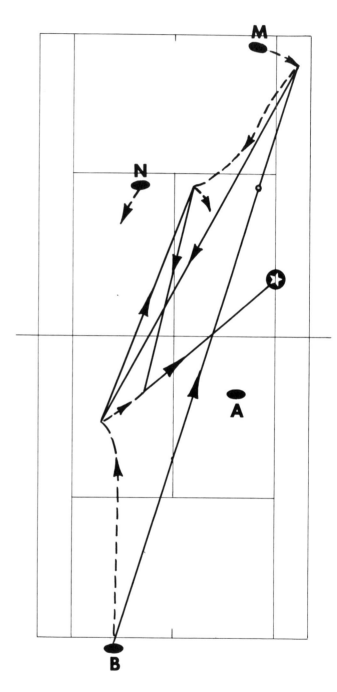

Figure 56

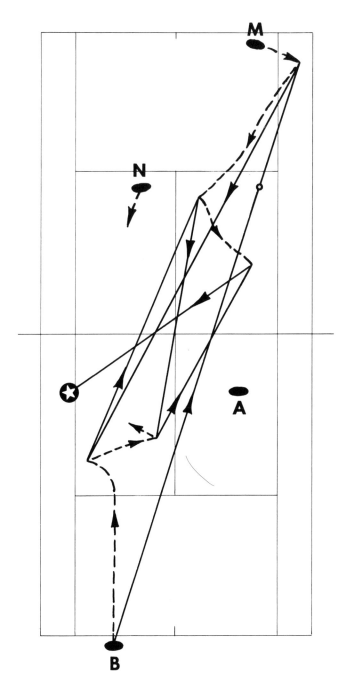

Here we have a point that begins as in Figure 56, but the server brings disaster down upon himself by being two steps late at every juncture. His first volley has to be hit up a bit as he strokes the return of service nearer the end of its flight. This permits receiver **M** to get in a step further, so that the return volley must be played from near the middle of the service court by server **B**. Since **B** cannot get a sharp angle on his volley, it becomes a simple matter for receiver **M** to keep boring in, and to turn the tables by angle volleying himself for a crisp placement. What a difference two steps can make in the outcome of a point!

Figure 57

This is a splendid example of a net duel ending in a sudden-death angle volley. The duel was between Jack Kramer and Frank Sedgman in a match that pitted Kramer and Segura against Sedgman and McGregor.

Server Kramer, **B,** took receiver Sedgman's, **M,** return of service in close to the net and volleyed to the center at Sedgman's feet. When Sedgman angled his return volley slightly, Kramer started angle volleying back. With each exchange Kramer's cute sliced backhand volleys forced Sedgman further and further off the court; and net man **A,** Segura, prevented Sedgman from slipping one down the line by carefully guarding the alley. Finally, since his partner's side was empty, modified net man McGregor, **N,** made a move to cover the middle of the court. Kramer spotted McGregor's move immediately and angled a neat volley in back of him for a great point.

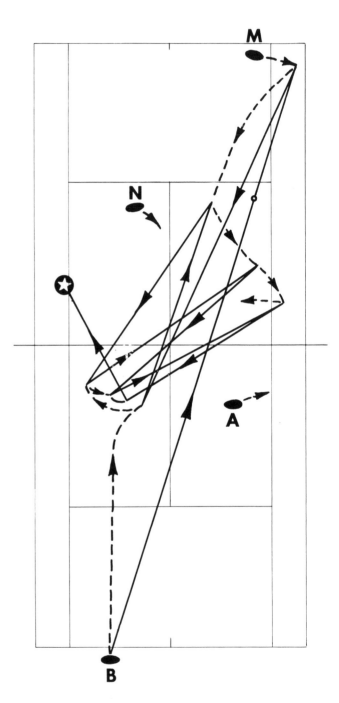

Figure 58

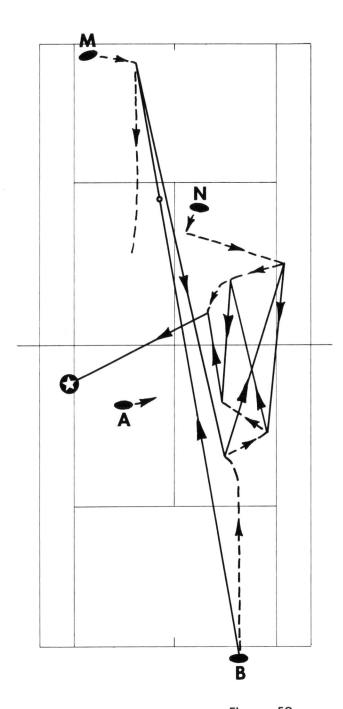

Another net exchange ending in an angle volley for the point, as executed by a fine modified net player.

Server **B** almost won the point on his excellent first volley down the line. But modified net man **N** anticipated the shot soon enough to change direction, lunge, and barely get the ball back. Server **B** thought he could win by hitting again at off-balance player **N**. But **N** scrambled back rapidly and returned a cute, soft volley at the feet of server **B**. This forced **B** to volley up, so player **N** moved in on top of the net and triumphantly angle volleyed past net man **A** for the point.

Figure 59

This shows a really sensational angle volley by one of the better angle-volley artists, Australian Mervyn Rose.

Server **B** tried to go for a placement on his sharply angled first volley. However, receiver **M** saw what was coming and covered the shot after a good run. Meanwhile net man **A**, Rose, had noted the server's bounce point and floated to his own right. But now that receiver **M** was ready to play a ground stroke from off the court, Rose had to decide how to cover the unguarded alley. His first impulse was to dash directly over. But when he saw receiver **M** was still uncommitted as to his return, Rose hesitated purposely at point **C** shown on the diagram. This maneuver drew **M** into playing down the seemingly unguarded alley. Once **M** had committed himself, Rose dashed for the sideline and whipped a gorgeous left-handed angle volley across the width of the court for the point.

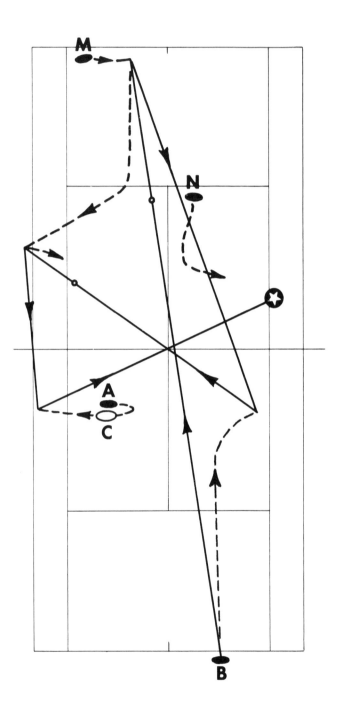

Figure 60

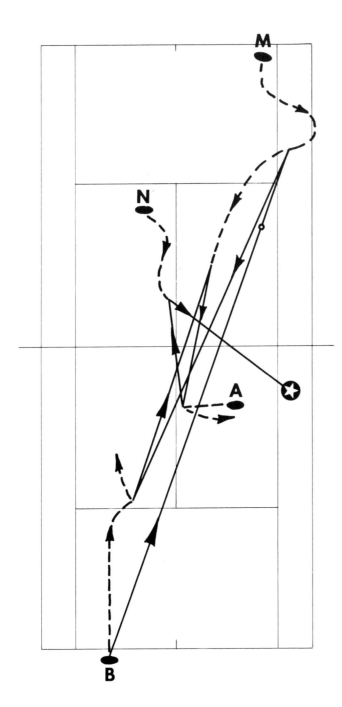

This is Australian power doubles at its unmerciful best, demonstrated by Sedgman and McGregor.

The lesson here is how to overwhelm a slightly shallow second serve. Receiver Sedgman, **M,** moves way in on the second serve and runs around the ball to play a hard-topped forehand return of service on the rise. The shot catches server **B** on the way in, at about the service line, and forces him to volley up from that deep position. Like a big cat, Sedgman moves in on top of the net and volleys low to the middle at the feet of net man **A.** Now Sedgman and McGregor sense the only return net man **A** can make will be hit up, and must pass over the net near its midpoint. They pack the center so closely that they can reach out and shake hands. Then modified net man, McGregor, **N,** reaches out and nonchalantly applies the crusher—a sharp-angle volley, which is gone before the opponents can move.

Figure 61

This angle volley by server **B** would be called perfect all the way from Wimbledon to Melbourne. The key to the play is the server's run all the way in to net, so that he could volley down and put some pace on his angle shot. For what can happen if he does not, see Figure 63.

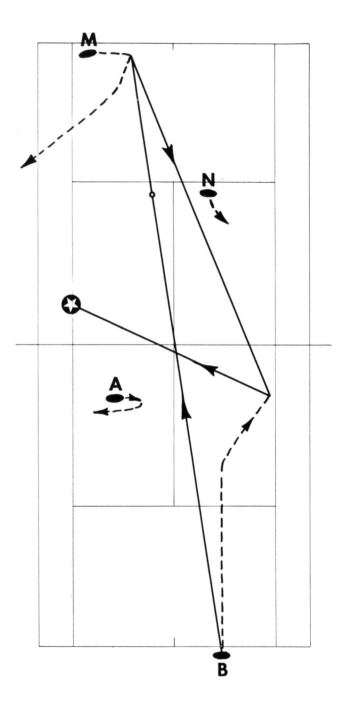

Figure 62

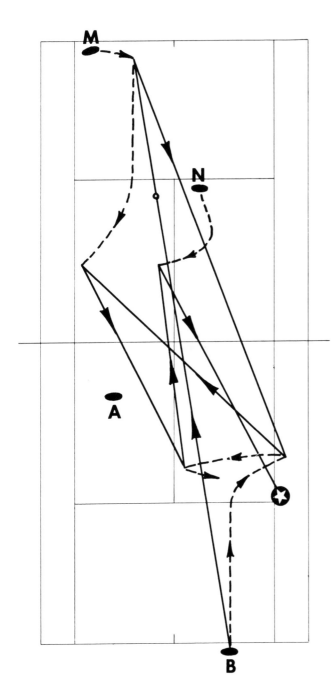

This point begins the same way as the one in Figure 62, but server **B** is slower moving in, so that his angle volley has to be hit up. Receiver **M** now has time to move in fast after his return of service and volley back low to the center. Modified net man **N** sizes up the situation and anticipates that server **B** will probably play his low backhand volley down the center. So player **N** wisely moves up, floats to the center, cuts off the return volley, and angle volleys for a placement. *Moral:* The server cannot afford to waste any time getting in to net.

Figure 63

Here we see Trabert and Seixas using the angle volley to take advantage of poor position play by modified net man **N**.

Server Trabert, **B**, makes the standard first volley to the middle. Receiver **M** notices that Seixas, **A**, has floated over to the center, so he tries to slip an angle volley down the sideline. But Seixas moves back quickly and at the same time sees that modified net man **N** is slow in moving in toward the net. So Seixas pulls out of his bag of tricks a sliced angle volley and plays the shot cross-court at a startling angle. You could actually hear the fuzz come off the ball with a resounding swoosh on this shot.

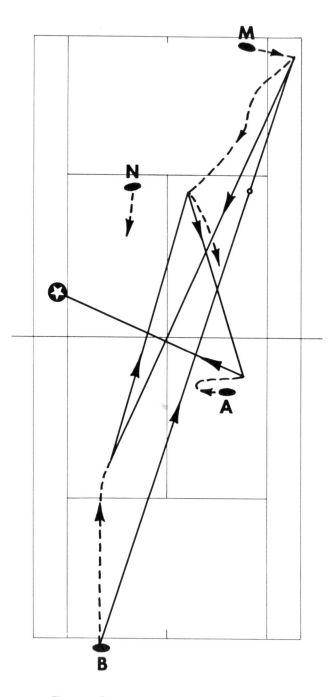

Figure 64

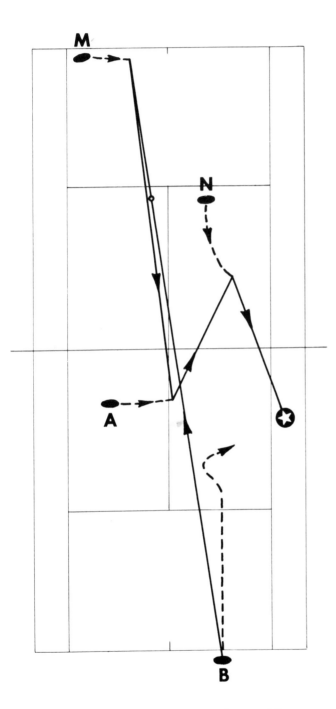

In contrast to Figure 64, we see here a nimble modified net man turn the tables on the serving team.

Receiver **M** has hit a return high to the middle. It permits net man **A** to float to the center and angle off a volley for what appears to be an easy winner. But modified net man **N** has carried out his assignment of watching net man **A** for any sign of a poach, and is able to anticipate what is coming. Player **N** moves up and over to cover the area. He is handsomely rewarded with a chance to angle volley past server **B**, who was drawn to the center, for the point.

Figure 65

The key player in this point is net man **A**. Server **B** has made the standard first volley to the middle at the feet of receiver **M** as **M** follows in after his return of service. Net man **A** anticipates that receiver **M** will volley up to the middle. So he moves up toward the center and has an easy angle volley to either side for the point.

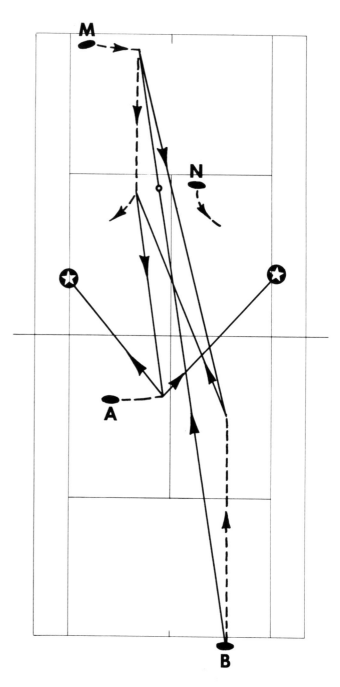

Figure 66

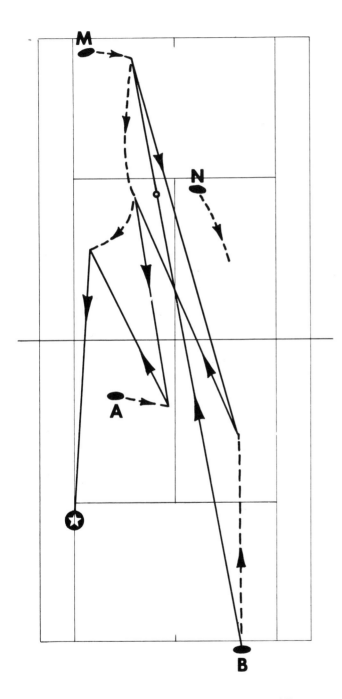

Figure 67

This point begins exactly the same way as that shown in Figure 66. But this time net man **A** is slow in moving toward the center, and he has to run back slightly to get to the ball. Thus his angle volley loses some of its sting, and receiver **M** just has enough time to dash in and pound a nice deep volley down the line for the point. Once again a step or two determines which team will win the point.

Overhead Play

It is axiomatic that the player with the stronger overhead should play the backhand court, so that he can take lobs down the center on his forehand overhead side. The axiom was never more dramatically —or amusingly—demonstrated than in the spring season in 1933, when Bitsy Grant, all of five feet five inches tall, teamed with powerful Lester Stoefen, who was exactly one foot taller. They made the greatest Mutt and Jeff team of all time, and they were mighty successful, as Bitsy's soft, tantalizing shots forced the opponents to hit up to the powerful giant. In fact, Stoefen got the habit of poaching for the overhead kills so far over on Bitsy's side that "the mighty atom" rebelled good-naturedly in an early round match at Pinehurst.

Bitsy complained volubly that he had not been allowed to hit an overhead all day. It didn't work: Stoefen, in a clowning mood, used one hand to push Bitsy aside as he yelled, "Mine," and smashed away overhead after overhead on lobs hit in Bitsy's direction. Finally Bitsy decided he would hit one if it killed him. As the giant started to poach on the next lob, Bitsy grabbed Stoefen's racquet arm and actually shinnied up the tall guy's frame to hit his first and only overhead. Everyone cheered—the crowd and all four players.

In normal practice each man takes care of lobs hit in his direction and refrains from crossing over too far, which would leave his team out of position. There are three exceptions to this normal practice, however. On short lobs a player may cross over slightly when it permits him to smash at a greater angle for the placement. This move is especially effective if the player happens to be a step or so nearer the net than his partner. The second exception: when one man has been forced in close to the net, and the opponents lob over his head, his partner must anticipate the situation and be prepared to drop back to take the overhead. In both cases the partners should call, "Yours," or, "Mine," to avoid getting in each other's way, and to help each other to take the best defensive position for a return of the smash. (These and other overhead plays are shown in Figures 68 through 73.) The final exception: when the sun is at a bad angle for one partner, or the wind is causing a bad cross-court drift. Here real teamwork is necessary.

Good overhead play requires skill in hiding intent until the last moment, for good anticipation and retrieving ability by the opponents can turn outright winners into lost opportunities. It also calls for a knowledge of the position of the opponents at the instant the stroke is made. The competent overhead player always notes the movement as well as the position of the opponents just before making his shot. Nothing can make him feel more foolish than hitting a resounding smash to "open" territory, only to find an alert defender waiting for the ball; for if he had taken more careful notice, he could have put the ball away easily—by changing the direction and catching the defender moving the wrong way. Too often the player persists in whaling the devil out of the ball, to no avail, when by simply and safely blocking the overhead to the proper spot he would have won the point. A cool head is just as valuable under temptation as under fire. The great overhead artists like Quist seldom made the stroke any better than it had to be to win the point. They cared little whether it drew the "Ohs" and "Ahs" of the gallery.

Developing a reliable overhead is of vital importance in doubles. Although the stroke is used rather infrequently (as shown in Table IV), the overhead accounts for about 14 per cent of all the winners (Table V) and leads all strokes in lethality (Tables VI and VIII). Clearly, when the opponents are put on the defensive and must resort to the lob, there is usually a good opportunity to smash for a point; and it is a shame to miss out on such opportunities for the lack of necessary stroke equipment. It is a pleasure to be able to report, for a change, that this is one phase of doubles in which the United States excels. Men like Doeg, Budge, Vines, Richards, Stoefen, Tilden, Schroeder, Gonzales, and Kramer had overhead smashes that left little to be desired. Consider, too, the psychological impact of the overhead. No stroke is more satisfying to make successfully; but nothing is more discouraging to one's partner, after he has struggled to maneuver the opponents into tossing up a weak lob, than to stand by expectantly and then watch his teammate flub the kill. Fortunately, the overhead is one of the easiest strokes to practice. Doubles partners should make a habit of tossing lobs to one another to perfect their overheads; and on the day of a match they should check both the wind and the sun to assure good overhead play.

It is interesting to study the overhead tactics of the top players. In general they play the point in the surest manner—by hitting the first overhead safely deep to the center of the court to draw the opponents together, then hitting the return lob away with a sharp angled overhead for the placement. (Two such plays are shown in Figures 68 and 70.)

If the first lob can be played within the service court, the striker should try for the placement on the first overhead. The same is true if the opponents are caught out of position. (Examples of this are given in Figures 69 and 73.)

This is a typical angled overhead winner. Server **B** has hit his first volley deep to the center and receiver **M** elects to lob deep. This forces net man **A** back. He circles under the lob and decides to hit his overhead safely down the middle. As soon as receiver **M** lobs again, server **B** realizes the lob will be short. At the same time he sees he has a better angle open to him for a forehand overhead, so he calls for the ball, crosses over, and puts away a hard-angled overhead smash.

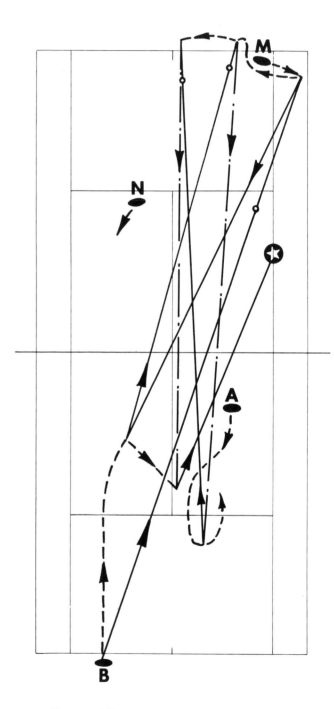

Figure 68

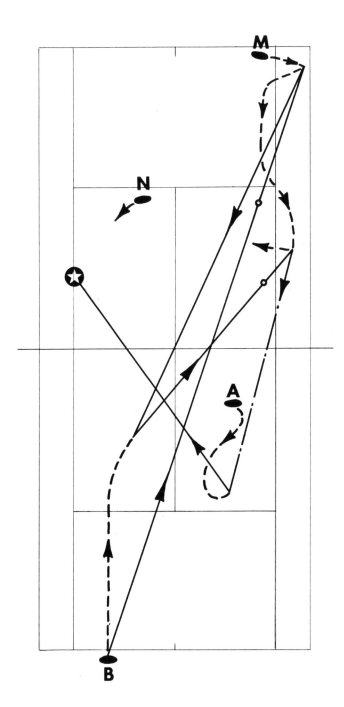

Here is an all-too-common
example of the short lob, and
the disaster that often results.
Server **B** has hit his first volley short and wide, which
gives receiver **M** a good
chance to lob. But the lob is
not aimed along the longest
dimension of the court, and
it is short. So net man **A** falls
back as the lob is about to be
played, and is able to hit
away an easy angled forehand
overhead for the point.

Figure 69

This shows nearly perfect overhead play by server **B**.

Receiver **M** lobs his return of service deep in an attempt to catch the server coming in too fast. However, server **B** has anticipated the lob in time to reverse his direction and play an overhead. Since the lob is beyond the service line he elects to play his overhead safe and deep down the middle (rather than gambling on putting it away). Receiver **M** covers the shot and again returns a well-hit, deep lob. Once more server **B** patiently plays his overhead deep down the middle. This time the return lob is short. Having drawn the opponents to the center, player **B** can now run in and smash an angled overhead to either side for a placement. Sound tactics, well executed.

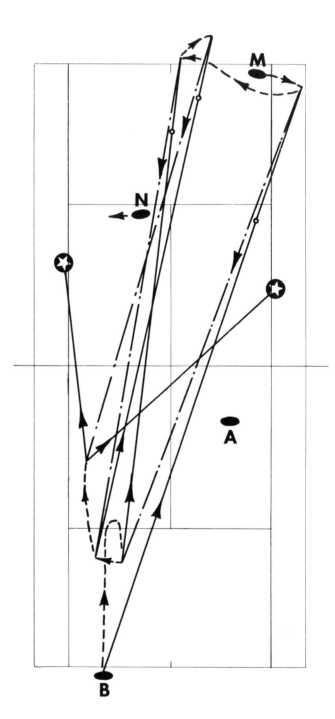

Figure 70

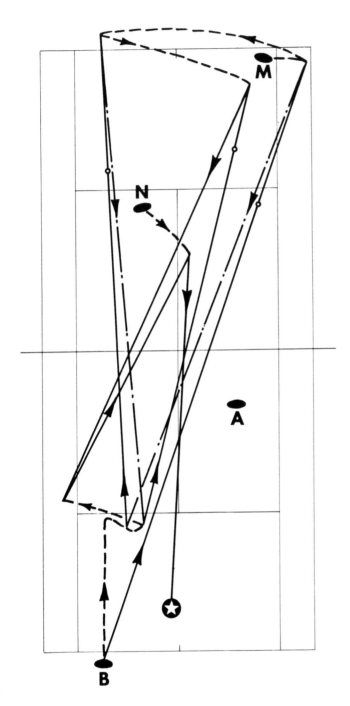

This play shows how a stubborn defense by Mulloy and Talbert was able to overcome poor overhead tactics used by Candy and Rose.

Receiver Mulloy, **M**, returns service with a medium depth lob. Server **B** gives away the direction of his overhead and does not hit it quite deep enough. Mulloy is able to call for the ball and run across the base line back of his partner and lob back fairly deep. Server **B** again fails to take advantage of his opening. He not only "telegraphs" the shot but hits a shallow overhead at an easy angle. Mulloy, **M**, scrambles back and plays a fine, low-topped cross-court backhand ground stroke, forcing server **B** to volley up from near the service line. Modified net man **N**, Talbert, then is able to intercept the shot and volley deep through the middle for the point.

Figure 71

This figure shows alert team play by net man **A**.

After making his first volley to the center, server **B** is drawn wide by a soft-angle volley stroked by receiver **M**. Server **B** replies with a soft-angle volley and moves toward the net for the kill. But receiver **M** crosses him up by hitting a lob volley toward the corner of the server's side of the court. Fortunately, net man **A** anticipates the shot, drops back to cover for his partner, notes the position of his opponents, and blocks a deep backhand overhead between them for the point. This is the kind of a partner to have!

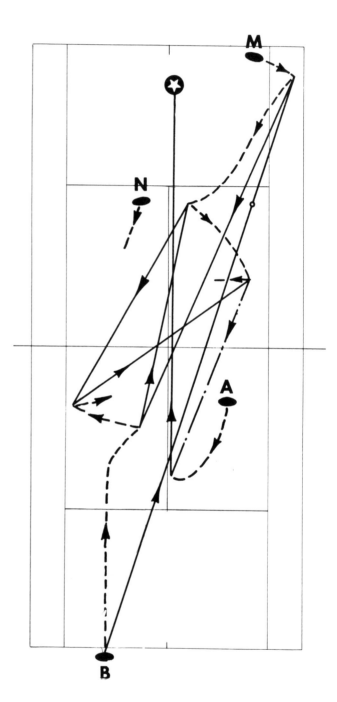

Figure 72

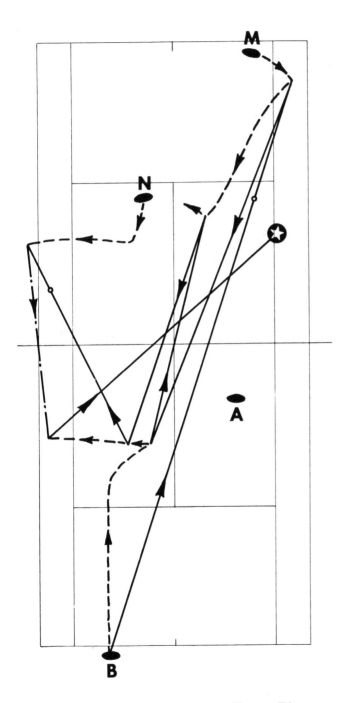

Figure 73

This time the ladies show us a brilliant point. It occurred in a match between Brough and Dupont, and Hart and Fry.

Miss Brough, **B,** serves and hits her first volley to the middle. Receiver Hart, **M,** volleys back just too low for Brough to put away her sharply angled return volley. As the alert modified net player Fry, **N,** runs to cover, she decides to hit a lob down the line in order to gain enough time to get back to position. But Brough anticipates the shot, sweeps the court, notices Hart moving to cover the center, moves to her own left at the proper moment, jumps, and hits a lovely angled backhand overhead for the point.

If the lob is played so well that it must be bounced, it should be hit deep with a severe stroke similar to a flat serve. It is often possible in this case, as well as with conventional overhead smashes, for the partner of the striker to move toward the center of the net and poach effectively against a weak return. Allison and Van Ryn employed this play many times to advantage. It is particularly useful when the striker is between the service line and the base line and may not have time to get well back in to the net before the return (see Figure 93).

The Soft and the Drop Volley

The soft volley and the drop, or stop, volley are important parts of the stroke repertoire. The soft volley is usually employed to force a weak return during volleying exchanges when all four players are at net. The drop volley is used to gain a placement when the opposing team is out of position.

When all four players are at net, and the opponents have the better offensive position closer to the net, a low soft volley at or near their feet often catches them off guard and forces them to hit up a weak return, thus opening the door for a kill. Change of pace, properly applied, is a very powerful weapon.

The soft volley comes in handy in another way. If a well-placed shot by the foe is about to sail past for a placement, and the net man must lunge for the ball, he frequently has no choice but to hit a soft volley. This desperation defense keeps the ball low and slows the pace until the net man has time to recover and get back into proper position.

The success of the drop volley depends on putting together the proper combination of touch and deception. It is used most effectively when one or both of the opponents are on the base line or moving rapidly toward an incorrectly anticipated point of return. In order to make the shot irretrievable, the striker must play it just over the net and impart to it a stiff spin so it bounces dead, like a lead ball. The perfect drop volley is tennis artistry of the highest order. It demands accurate control of the head of the racquet, which must give with the stroke to slow the ball down. If the shot is somewhat less than perfect the ball can be dumped into the net or just deep enough for one of the opponents to drive it past from close range. Either way, chalk up a quick point for the opposition! But delicately executed, especially on a slow court, the drop or stop volley will have the opponents breaking their backs trying to retrieve the ball. After a rainy week at a grass court tournament this shot is absolutely sensational—no bounce at all!

Diagrams of various soft and drop volley situations are shown in Figures 59, 82, and 74-77.

The Lob Volley

No stroke in tennis, singles or doubles, is as beautiful to behold, or as difficult to execute, as the lob volley. And nothing is more heartwarming to an inveterate doubles player than scoring a placement with a lob volley. It is a shot usually made when in difficulty, and to win with it is rather like the thrill that comes from holing out from a deep sand trap!

Assume all four players are at the net. Picture the opponents working their way in closer to the net, into a better offensive position with each volley. Then one of the opposing gentlemen hits a low volley at you and, overeager for the kill, one or both of the opponents move in too close to the net. Here is the crucial moment—one that demands quick thinking and a desperate move to prevent disaster. The proper diagnosis, a deft flick of the forearm and wrist, and up floats the loveliest of lobs, just out of reach of the off-balance opponents. In full view of the gallery the ball seems almost to pause there over the heads of the dismayed opponents, then continues its majestic parabola toward the base line for the point.

Success of this sort is really threading the needle under pressure, and giving the opposition a polite raspberry in the bargain. But, a lob volley hit too high is easily retrieved, and one hit too low will be blasted back for an easy point. The stroke, therefore, requires championship timing, touch, and surprise in order to produce a placement. The data recorded in Table VII show exactly how delicate this shot is: only 1 per cent of the winners and 1 per cent of the placements are made with the lob volley. George Lott and Frankie Parker were prime exponents of this stroke, and used it with telling effectiveness. It is a good weapon for the club player to use, for it will prevent his opponents from crowding the net too much. (Figures 78 through 82 illustrate the typical plays, offensive and defensive, involving the lob volley.)

Once again the ladies, Brough, Dupont, Hart and Fry, show us how tennis should be played. Miss Brough, **B,** serves perfectly to receiver Miss Hart, **M,** takes the net, and makes a fine first volley to the middle at the feet of receiver **M.** Miss Hart notices that server **B** is following her first volley in to an overpowering position at net, so that almost any return Hart makes would result in a crisp volley being hit back by Brough for the point. In fact, the situation looks hopeless. But Hart, **M,** decides cleverly to play a soft volley just over the net, hoping that it would compel Brough, **B,** to volley up defensively. This she did, and Brough was forced to volley up cross-court as Fry, **N,** had moved in to cover the net in front of her. Hart, **M,** anticipated what was coming, moved up very fast, cut off the return, and volleyed deep down the line for a beautifully executed and well-earned point.

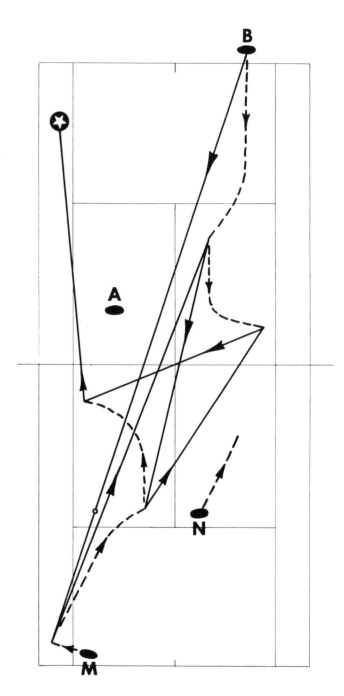

Figure 74

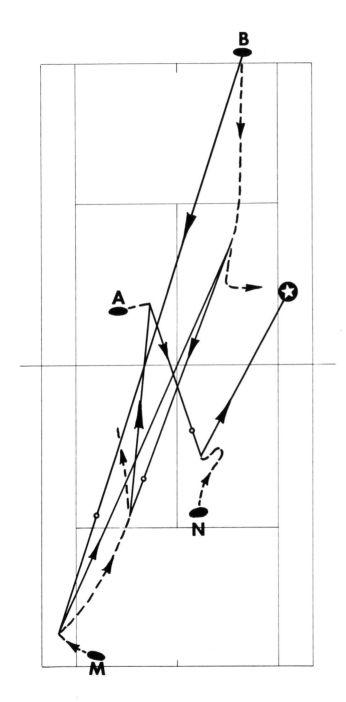

In contrast to Figure 74, this play shows how a soft volley can backfire if hit too shallow.

The first volley by server **B** is short, so that receiver **M** plays a low ground stroke to the middle to force net man **A** to volley up. As net man **A** prepares to make his shot, he notices modified net man **N** moving in to the net. So net man **A** decides to hit a soft volley at the feet of player **N**, thus forcing him to volley up. But the volley is just a bit too shallow; player **N** reverses his direction rapidly, so that he can let the ball bounce and play an offensive ground stroke. It works. Player **N** hits a topped backhand drive to the aim point for a winner.

Figure 75

Here is a classic drop volley. Server **B** has hit a deep first volley that pins receiver **M** on the base line and forces him to play a ground stroke from deep court. Net man **A**, sensing his opportunity, closes the center and notices that modified net man **N** is holding his original position. Therefore, net man **A** cleverly dumps a perfectly executed drop volley to the totally unguarded area for an easy point.

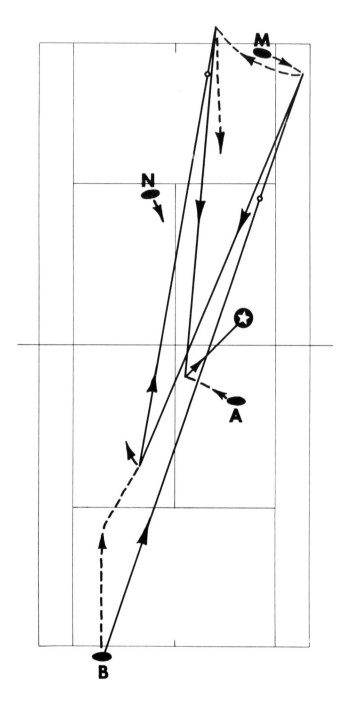

Figure 76

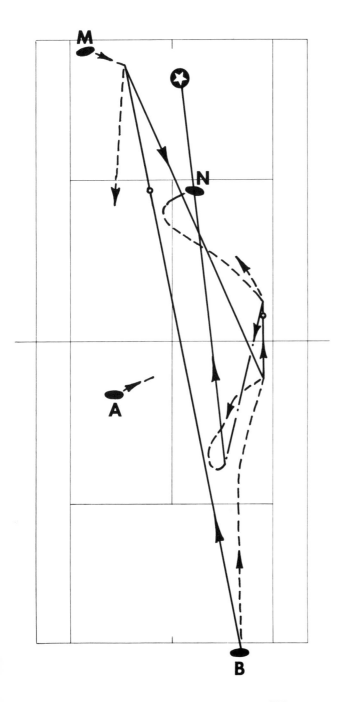

This is a good example of how a drop volley can set the stage for winning a point.

Receiver **M** has made such an excellent dink return of service that modified net man **N**, anticipating a first volley hit up cross-court, decides to cross over. But server **B**, on seeing this move, decides instead to cross up the defense and play a drop volley just over the net. Modified net man **N** sees this coming in the nick of time, reverses direction, and scrambles to reach the ball at the last second. Players **A** and **B** both note that player **N** will have to hit the ball up, so **A** moves to crowd the net and **B** drops back in anticipation of a weak lob dug out of the ground. This is exactly what happens, and server **B** smashes a deep overhead for the point.

Figure 77

This diagram shows the lob volley properly executed during a difficult point by the offensive team. Server **B** volleys the return of service properly at the feet of receiver **M** as he advances. Receiver **M** volleys back low and soft, and continues to move into the net. Server **B** continues his attempt to force receiver **M** to volley up by returning a soft volley at his feet. But receiver **M** artfully counters this by hitting back still another soft volley at server **B**'s feet; and then he and his partner, modified net man **N**, crowd the net ready to murder any return hit up by server **B.** In this desperate situation server **B** fakes another soft volley and then tosses up a deep lob volley to the base line for the point.

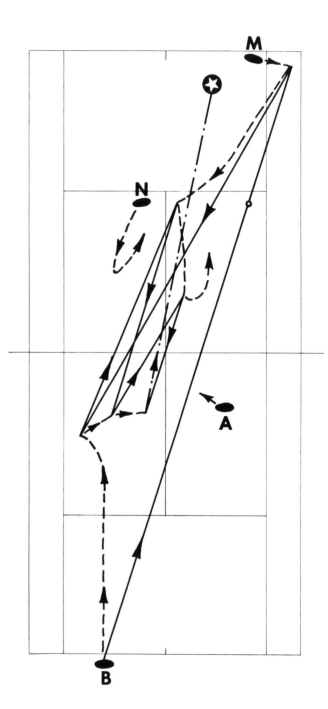

Figure 78

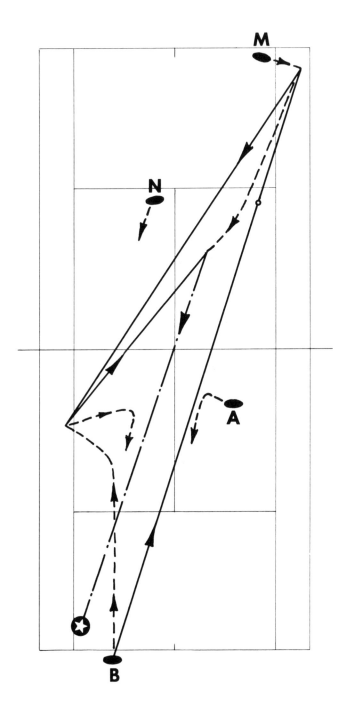

The use of the lob volley in this point shows one of the favorite tactics used by the expert dink shot player to engineer a service break.

Server **B** is forced to run way in to net to dig a dink shot out of the turf, and then he dashes to cover the center. Receiver **M** follows in rapidly behind his dink, notices that the opponents are close to the net and that server **B** is in motion toward the center. This gives **M** the opening he is looking for, and he lifts a firm lob volley just out of reach of server **B**, deep to the corner of the court for the point.

Figure 79

It doesn't take much to make the lob volley boomerang.

This point shows clever play by modified net man **N**. He sees that server **B** faces a difficult first volley of a good dink return of service by his partner **M**. Therefore, **N** fakes a move to the center to cut off a cross-court return. This fake causes server **B** to change his mind, and he hits a lob volley down the line. But player **N** anticipates the shot, dashes back, gets under the lob, and hits a fine overhead smash through the middle for the point. Note that player **M** is also moving to cover the lob if necessary.

All too often this is the fate of a lob volley that is hit too high or too low, or not well concealed.

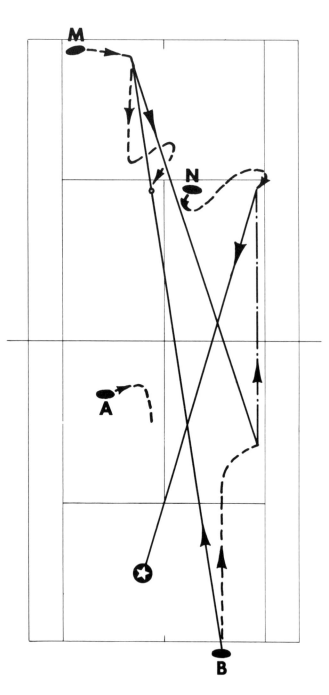

Figure 80

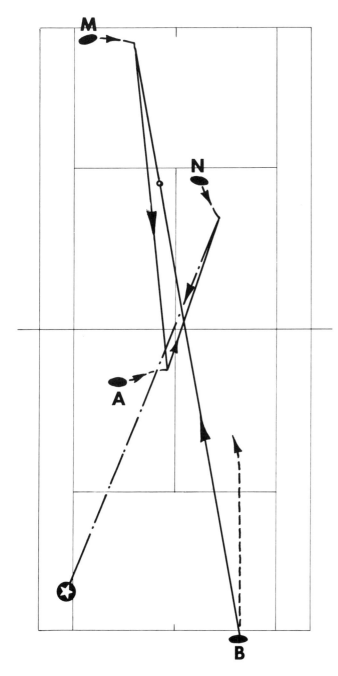

Figure 81

Here we have the desperation lob volley—even the guy who hit it would grin and admit it was half luck. But he deserves plenty of credit for his hair-trigger anticipation.

Receiver **M** hits a poor return of service high to the middle. Net man **A** moves over quickly to volley down crisply for what seems to be easy point. But modified net man **N** is, very properly, watching net man **A** carefully; and he moves to the spot where the volley should go. By keeping his racquet in front of him he is able to make a quick stab in the right direction and dump a lob volley neatly over the head of startled net man **A** for a placement.

Saves like this one build up the morale of the receiving team and tend to upset the equilibrium of the serving team.

This point shows a splendidly maneuvered service break by receiver **M**. He returns service near the middle and follows in to the net. Then he returns server **B's** first volley with that fine weapon, the soft-angled volley, to draw the server wide and force him to volley up defensively. Finally, as **M** sees server **B** rushing to the center, he catches him completely off balance by placing a lob volley over his outstretched racquet to the corner for the point.

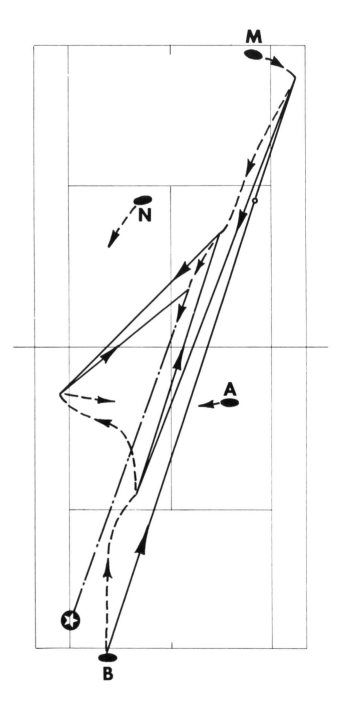

Figure 82

The Ground Strokes

In net play a short volley or ground stroke by the opponents often produces a bounding ball in the forward quarter of the court. What the net team should do in such circumstances is largely dictated by the height of the bounce.

If the bounding ball reaches the height of the net or higher, it is feasible to concentrate on winning the point outright. (Table VIII shows a high lethality for ground strokes hit down the line or at wide angles.) Such winners are brought off by punching hard, well-placed drives, flat or top spin, through holes in the opposition at point-blank range. Be certain you know where these holes are by observing the opponents' positions until the instant before you stroke the ball. A very high bounce should be played with an overhead, and many good players will actually crouch to get a chance to hit, with maximum power, an overhead on a bounce of intermediate height. If the opposition is near the base line, there is a chance to win by faking a drive and playing a delicate drop shot just over the net—not an easy maneuver.

On the other hand, a low-bouncing ball seldom opens up a chance to go after the point, and fencing usually follows. To draw the opposition out of position or force a weak return, the best weapons are the old reliable dink shot with spin to keep the bounce low, or the heavily topped shot. Wide angles or shots played at or near the feet of the opposing players are usually employed.

(Typical plays involving ground strokes from near the net are shown in Figures 83 through 88.)

The Poach

The poach is a vital maneuver in doubles play. It can be, and should be, a deadly maneuver; and what a comfort it is to have at net a partner who can pull off a successful poach for a placement at the right psychological moment!

Your partner's court should not be invaded unless it makes for a much more effective shot. In fact, the shot should have about a two-to-one chance of being a kill; otherwise the poach leaves your team out of position and presents an advantage to the enemy. Study of a match involving ace poachers showed that they produce close to the two-to-one ratio of points won against points lost, except on weak returns of first service, which they killed on about a four-to-one ratio.

This play might be called the sharp cross-court double-cross.

Server **B** volleys the return of service sharply cross-court and then starts to move in routine fashion toward the middle of his court. Receiver **M** comes up very fast to retrieve the ball, notes the incorrect position of server **B**, and hits a well-executed topped drive back sharply cross-court for the point.

In professional matches this type of exchange is often repeated with the ball getting closer and closer to the net until the crowd is in a frenzy before the ball is finally put away.

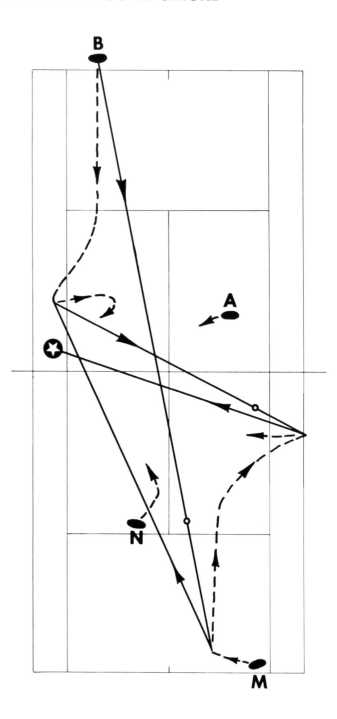

Figure 83

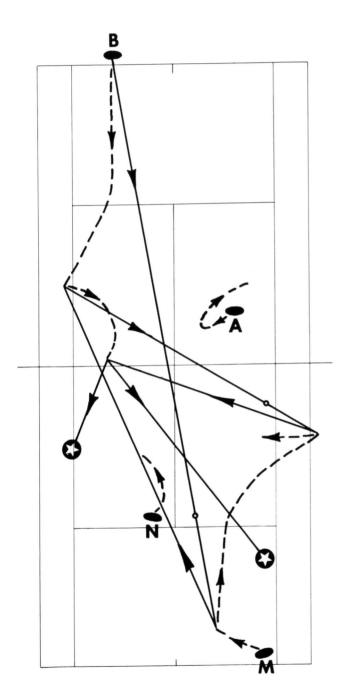

The sharp cross-court double-cross (Figure 83) can be easily thwarted if the partners play their positions properly.

Again we begin with a sharp cross-court first volley by server **B**; but this time **B** moves toward the net as well as toward the center, and net man **A** moves back and toward the sideline to present the best defensive formation (see also Figure 29). Thus it is easy for server **B** to move up, cut off the sharp cross-court return hit by receiver **M**, and volley to either of the two aim points for a winner.

Figure 84

This is a good example of how a forecourt ground stroke, backed by excellent team play, can win a point.

Server **B** makes a short first volley and attempts to compensate by continuing in to net rapidly, to be prepared for the return. Spotting the move, receiver **M** decides to let the short volley bounce to get better control of the ball for a delicate return. And control he certainly achieves: he slips a very soft, low-bouncing dink between server **B** and the net. Meanwhile modified net man **N** has been surveying the situation and has moved a couple of steps toward the net. As soon as he diagnoses the cross-court return of server **B**, he dashes way up and across court to bring off a great poach for the point.

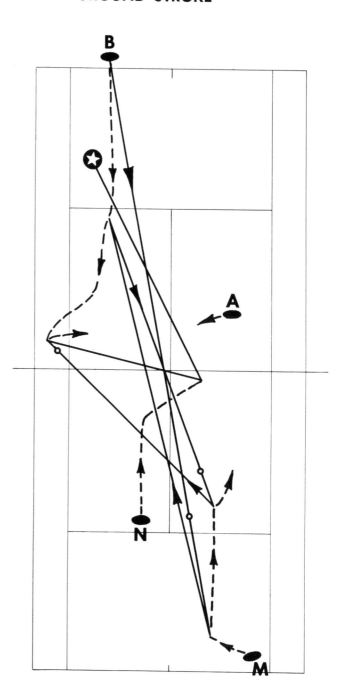

Figure 85

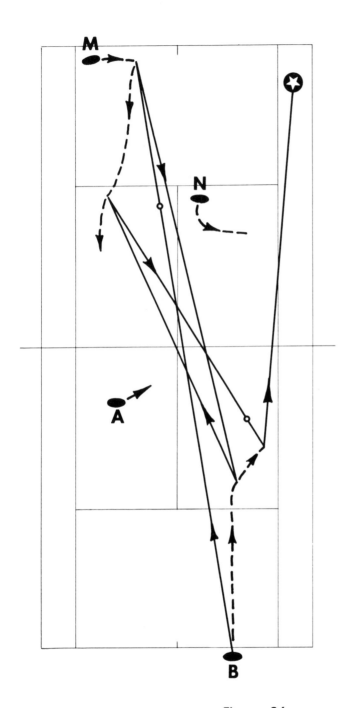

The forecourt ground stroke shown here is a simple one. Just remember to look over the court first, so that you drive the ball through the biggest and best opening.

Server **B** plays his first volley deep and forces receiver **M** to volley up short. Server **B** sees the ball will bounce high, so he waits for it while noting carefully the positions of the opponents. Then, seeing the cross court and center are well defended, he whistles a hard forehand drive down the sideline past **N** for the point.

This is the fate a short, high-bouncing volley often brings down upon your head (see Table VIII).

Figure 86

This diagram illustrates a perfect forecourt ground stroke.

The return of service by receiver **M** has drawn server **B** wide, from which spot **B** has played a shallow first volley to the middle. Modified net man **N** moves to cover the ball and, as he does so, sees that server **B** is moving to protect the expected down-the-center return. Instead, player **N** reaches out around the ball at the last moment and plays a beautifully angled, heavily topped drive to the alley for a placement.

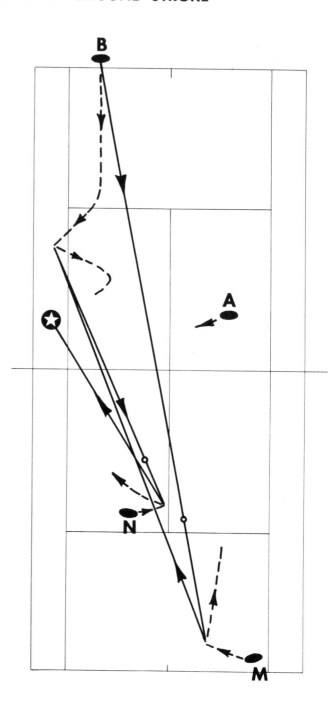

Figure 87

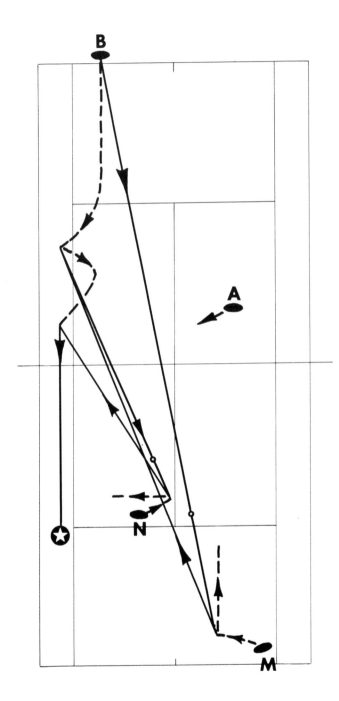

Here is the proper defense for the point shown in Figure 87. In this case server **B**, as he sees **N** reach out around the ball to play a topped, angled drive, slows his run to the middle and reverses direction. His keen anticipation pays off in an easy down-the-line volley for the point.

A comparison of Figures 87 and 88 shows clearly the importance of alertness, anticipation, and deception in top-notch doubles.

Figure 88

To be an expert poacher a player must have excellent anticipation and timing. It also helps to come equipped with speed, a long reach, and ability to volley for the kill. True artists like Tilden, Brugnon, Sedgman, Rose, Stoefen, and Seixas anticipate the point of return from careful study of the striker's habits, stance, and racquet; wait till the striker is fully committed; and then dash for the right spot (with a reach long enough to take care of any minor miscalculation) and volley forcefully for a placement. In week-end doubles a good poacher can confuse the opposition no end—fast men should try it more often.

In net play the poach serves two purposes—offensive and defensive. The so-called poach of opportunity covers all cases in which a player moves into his partner's territory to produce a placement or, at least, to play a stronger forcing shot or a better angle than his partner can. Often this can be done because the poacher is nearer the net and can volley down, or because his partner is slightly out of position. Also, a poach can enable one of the partners to bring his stronger forehand to bear, rather than leaving his partner to block back a weak backhand shot.

The defensive poach is a point-saving maneuver used when one's partner is hopelessly out of position. It usually involves a strategic delay—waiting till the last second to draw a shot to the uncovered area, then dashing to cover the spot which the opponents are likely to use as their aim point.

As a tactic the poach can be most unnerving to the opponents. It often turns what started out to be a good, well-placed shot by the striker into an easy point for the poacher. In addition, it forces the striker to watch the positions of the opposing team up to the last split second before shifting all his attention to hitting the ball: in many cases he allows a greater margin of safety than he ordinarily would— that is, he tries too hard to keep the ball clear of the potential poacher. Finally, the poach helps the good doubles player to mix up his game, so that his habits cannot be so easily detected or exploited by an expert poacher on the other side of the net.

The fake poach can be used effectively at intervals to divert the attention of the opponents or to draw a shot. With his partner hopelessly out of position, a player can sometimes save the point by purposely starting too soon to cover the exposed court area, then scrambling back to intercept a ball hit to the spot he guarded previously. In the 1954 National Doubles tourney the fake poach was used fairly often by the net man in an effort to upset the receiver when his partner was serving at advantage out.

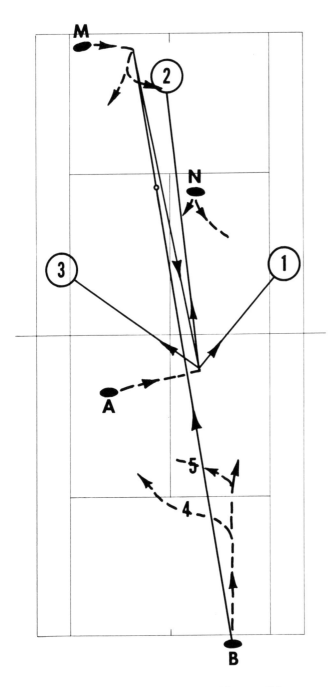

This diagram shows doubles' most commonly used poach. It is made by the net man after a strong first serve by his partner has drawn a weak cross-court return of service.

Net man **A** can make such poaches on his own or use the signaled poach. In either case his play is the same. He must hold his ground until the receiver is committed, then make his fast dash. Once he reaches the ball, he has three possible aim points, as shown. He should select his play depending on the defensive positions of the opposing team, and hit for the placement.

Server **B** comes up path 5 on an unsignaled poach, prepared either to cover the return of service if it gets by net man **A,** or to run to cover the unprotected side. On a signaled poach server **B** starts up the same path to fool the receiver, and then cuts over along path 4.

Figure 89

The defense against the poach play shown in Figure 91 should be set largely to cover aim points 1 and 2. Aim point 3 is used less frequently because it is the most difficult volley for net man **A** to make: he has to be able to reach ahead of the ball to volley it at that angle.

The defense against aim point 1 is the responsibility of net man **N.** If he watches net man **A** intently, anticipates, and moves to the proper spot, he has a fair chance of turning a lost cause into a point. Here we see **N** making perfect returns to aim point 6 or 7.

The defense against any other volley is up to receiver **M.** Volleys to aim point 2 are usually low and crisp, so that modified net player **N** would have a tough shot. He should let the ball go through to player **M,** who has a better chance at it. Thus receiver **M** should stay on the base line as he sees the poach develop, then be ready to cover aim points 2 or 3 as shown.

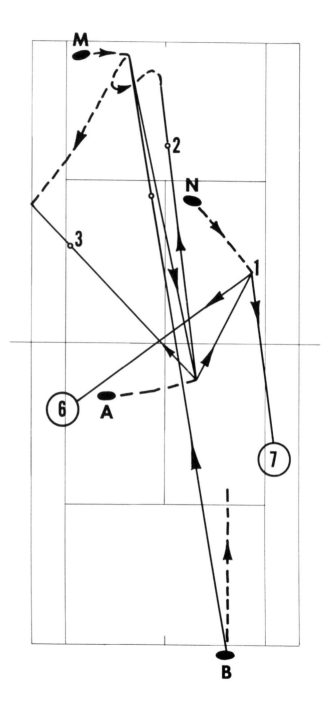

Figure 90

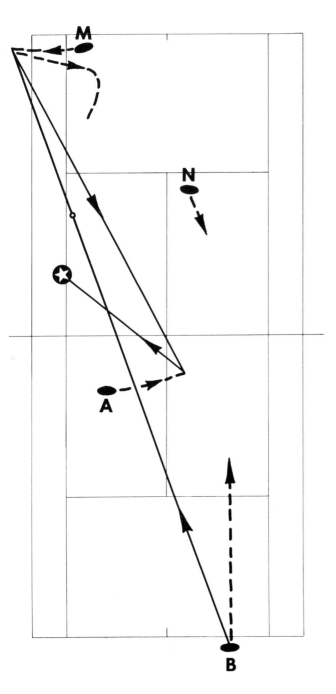

Figure 91

This is a very sweet poach as demonstrated by a very tough pair, Kramer and Segura.

A surprise slice serve by Kramer, **B**, runs receiver **M** way off the court and forces him into making a weak cross-court return of service. Net man **A**, Segura, waits until he is almost certain where the return will go, and then dashes along the net. As he prepares to stroke the volley, he sees that receiver **M** is running back along the base line toward the center of the court. Segura decides to catch **M** going the wrong way, so he angles a crisp volley to the left, hopelessly out of reach of **M**, for an easy placement.

A poorly executed poach can spell sudden death. This play begins as in Figure 91, but the volley by net man **A** is neither crisp enough nor angled sharply enough. This gives receiver **M** time to change direction, cover the ball, and drive a ground stroke down the line on the unguarded side for an easy placement.

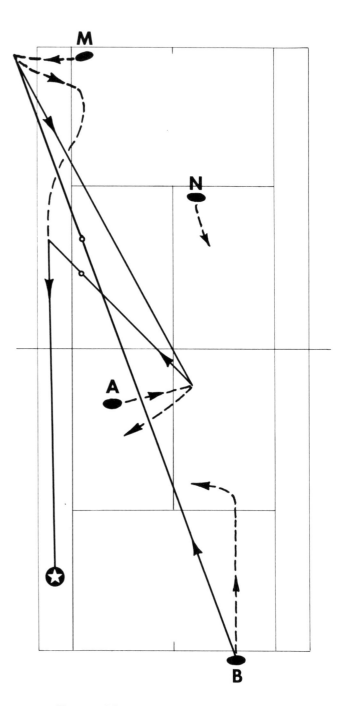

Figure 92

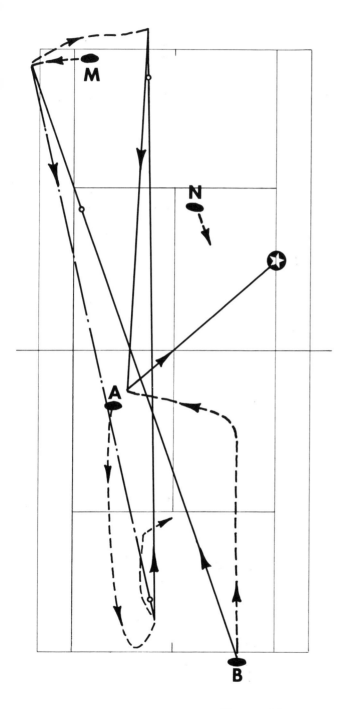

This diagram shows a favorite poach play of the celebrated team of Allison and Van Ryn.

Server **B** catches receiver **M** off balance with a slice serve to the corner. Receiver **M** elects to hit a high, deep, defensive lob return of service, which net man **A** (Van Ryn) decides to let bounce. Net man **A** then returns the high-bouncing ball with a hard overhead stroke down the middle, and heads back toward the net. Receiver **M** tries to take advantage by hitting a drive from the base line to the feet of player **A** as he comes in. Meanwhile, server **B**, Allison, has moved up to the net. He anticipates exactly what player **M** is attempting, holds his ground until **M** is committed, then executes a fast poach and angles off an easy volley for the point.

Figure 93

Here is never-say-die tennis as displayed by the 1952 U. S. National champions, Rose and Seixas, against Sedgman and McGregor in the finals of that tournament.

Receiver Sedgman, **M,** plays an effective dink return of service and advances to the net with his usual speed. This forces server Rose, **B,** to hit up, and he wisely plays a soft-angle volley. Net man Seixas, **A,** thinks this will compel Sedgman to volley back cross-court, so he starts for the middle to cut off the return. But Sedgman, **M,** crosses him up and dumps one down the alley. Sexias puts on the brakes, turns, makes a frantic dash, then dives for the ball. He just manages to return it but falls down flat in the process. Server Rose, **B,** stands calmly and watches Sedgman take careful aim down the line as Seixas struggles to get up. Then at the last second, with Sedgman committed, Rose makes a very fast defensive poach and volleys back miraculously. Sedgman is astounded. It's his turn to dive for one. But, despite the fact he has the whole court open to him for a placement, he can not *quite* get the ball back. Some tennis!

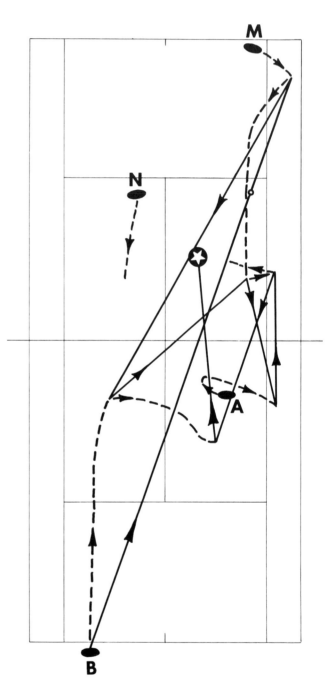

Figure 94

To make poaching most effective, a set of signals should be worked out between partners (see Figures 8, 9, and 10). Signals for a fake or planned poach are obviously helpful, but it is often impossible to signal for other poaches. The partner of the poacher, whether or not he receives a signal, must be prepared to have the ball come through to him past the poacher's outstretched racquet. Many points can be saved by carefully continuing to follow the flight of the ball, even though one's partner is crossing in front to attempt a poach.

One small note of warning: poaching can be overdone. Tilden was accused of overdoing it many times. Used to excess, poaching makes for poor doubles. It puts your team out of position too often and gives away your tactics. What is more, it is likely to be very trying on your partner. No one enjoys playing with a court-hog, and no doubles team can possibly be good without smooth teamwork and a solid understanding between partners.

(Several typical poaching plays are shown in Figures 89 through 94.)

The Drift

A smart variation of the poach, which we hereby name the drift, is very much in evidence whenever the Australians play. The drift is a play made at the net, and there are two versions of it: one for the serving team, one for the receiving team. (Both are depicted in Figures 95 through 98.)

For the serving team the drift is a maneuver wherein the net man, on anticipating a cross-court return of service, moves or drifts along the net toward the center of the court. This accomplishes the followings things: (1) it permits the server to come up wide to cover sharp angles, presenting a tight defense with two men in position to cover that half of the court to which the ball is being played; (2) it permits the net man to volley away returns hit down the middle; (3) it allows the net man to continue his drift into a poach if the return of service is weak and high; and (4) it puts tremendous pressure on the receiver, forcing him to watch the position of the net man more carefully and giving him a much smaller target to shoot at for an effective return of service. Thus, the drift will force many errors on the return of service.

For the receiving team the drift is made by the modified net man as the server gets set to make his first volley. As soon as the net man notes that the first volley will be played cross-court or hit up, he moves

Here is the drift play, used so effectively by the Australians to limit the area for safe returns of service by the receiver.

The drift is made by net man **A.** At the moment he anticipates a cross-court return of service by **M,** he drifts slightly forward and along the net to a point a step or so beyond the middle of the court. His partner, server **B,** can now come up to net wide, to cover sharply angled returns. This practically eliminates any chance for **M** to score a placement on his return of service, unless he has hidden his intentions so well that he can play his return down the line in back of net man **A.**

This maneuver puts such pressure on the receiver that it caused as fine a player as Seixas in the 1952 Nationals to sprinkle area **E** with errors trying to keep his return of service away from the drifting net man.

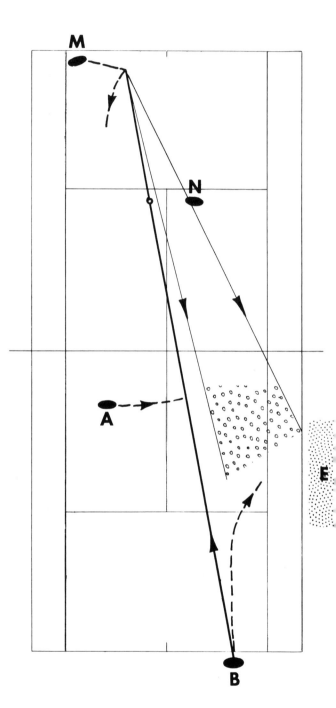

Figure 95

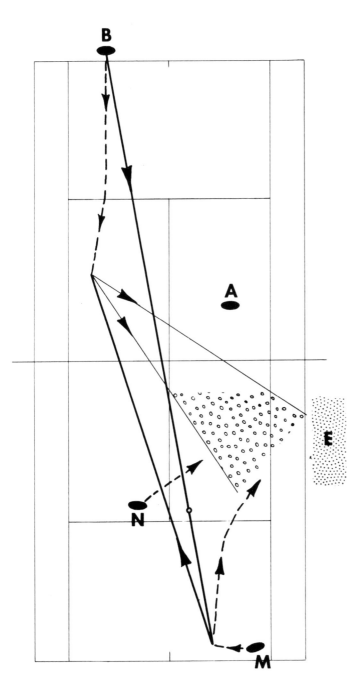

Here we have the drift play used by modified net man **N** to limit the area for a safe cross-court first volley by the server.

As soon as **N** sees that his partner's return of service is an effective one, and that server **B** is about to make the standard cross-court first volley, he starts to drift across the middle of the court and toward the net. This permits receiver **M** to come up wide to protect against sharply angled volleys, thus improving the court coverage of the receiving team.

This sort of psychological warfare by the receiving team causes many an expert to hit numerous first volleys into the net (trying to keep them low enough so that **N** cannot volley effectively), and to spatter area E with errors (trying to keep the ball out of reach of the receiving team).

Figure 96

This play is a prime favorite of ace Australian doubles players Sedgman and Rose.

Receiver **M** has made an effective return of service, using a dink or a topped drive, which forces server **B** to volley up. This brings joy to the heart of a fast modified net man like Sedgman, **N**. After anticipating a cross-court return, he drifts forward and across the court and finally dashes for the proper spot to volley down savagely to aim point 1 or 2 for the point. This is really good fun!

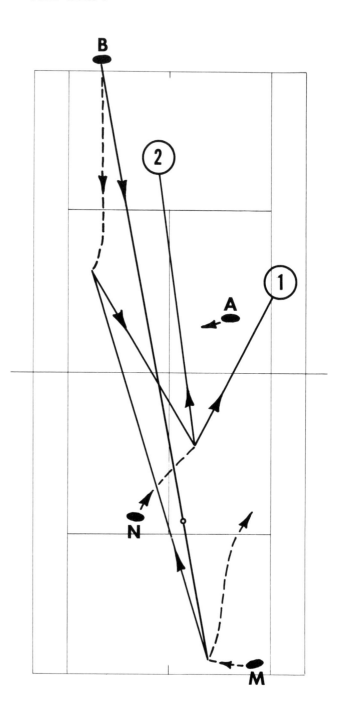

Figure 97

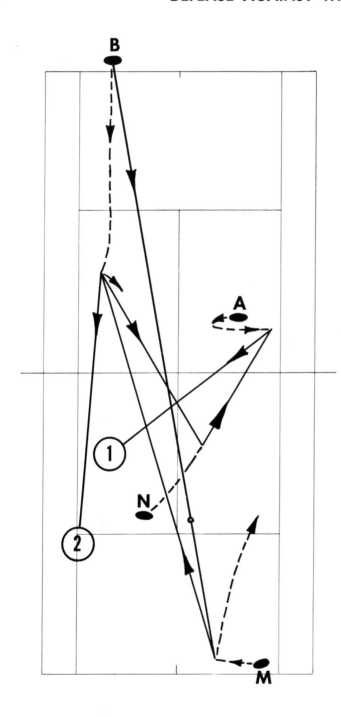

Figure 98

The serving team can ruin the drifting team's fun if they keep their wits about them.

Server **B** should note carefully whether modified net man **N** is starting to drift. If he detects the drift soon enough, he can dump any old volley down the line to aim point 2 and win the point. If server **B** does not detect the drift until he is committed to a cross-court volley, **B** should keep his first volley low. This takes the sting out of modified net man **N**'s return volley by forcing him to hit up. Now net man **A** comes into the play. He has, quite correctly, been watching modified net man **N.** So he moves to the proper spot and angle volleys the return to the wide-open spaces at aim point 1 for a fine placement.

This is a clever draw play made by Doris Hart in the finals of the U. S. Nationals in 1954 against Brough and Dupont.

Miss Brough, **M**, makes an excellent dink return of service, which forces Miss Hart, **B**, to hit up a short first volley that bounces high inside the service court. Hart sees that receiver Brough has moved up: Brough has an easy forehand shot which she can place through the hole in the middle or behind Hart if she runs to cover the middle too soon. Therefore, Hart elects to remain at point C until she has drawn the shot down the middle. Then she dashes to close the gap and angles off a beautiful volley to win a point almost certainly lost.

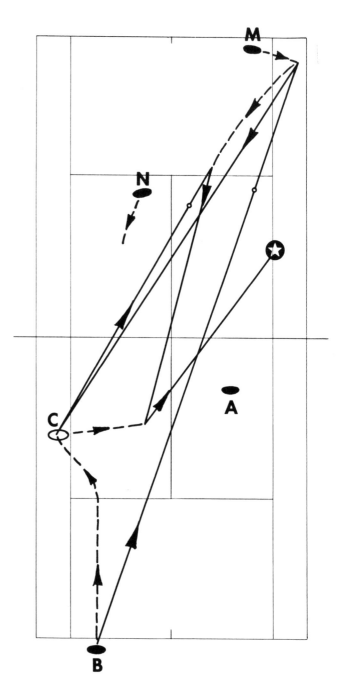

Figure 99

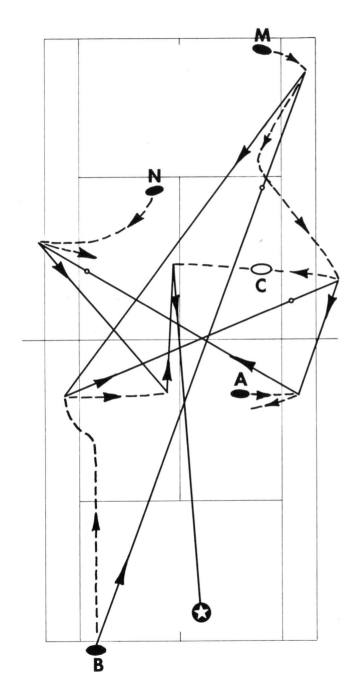

Figure 100

During the 1954 U. S. Nationals final this superb desperation draw play was made by the great little Rosewall.

Seixas, **B**, serves. At once he sees that the return of service by Rosewall, **M**, is high. So Seixas runs well in to the net and angles off a sharp volley that almost wins the point outright. But Rosewall guesses what's coming and, after a hard run, he retrieves the ball. He tries to slip his return down the line past net man **A**, Trabert, but Trabert has anticipated the shot so well that he is able to angle volley all the way cross-court for what looks like a winner. This time modified net man **N**, Hoad, saves the situation by running rapidly to. the sideline. He tries to hit back through the middle between Seixas and Trabert. But Seixas has anticipated this shot and, with the Aussies hopelessly out of position, he moves over to pound the ball down the empty center of the court for a "sure winner." However, Rosewall, **M**, has other ideas. He had scrambled back as far as point C when he detected Seixas' intention. He hesitates at point C until Seixas is fully committed, then sprints to cover the shot and volley deep down the middle for the point!

across the center line and toward the net. This gives his team these advantages: (1) it permits the modified net man to volley away many weak first volleys; (2) it provides a better defense, for the receiver can come up wide to cover the sharply angled volley; and (3) by forcing the server to thread the needle with his first volley, it often teases him into making errors.

Basically, the whole idea of the drift is to take advantage of cross-court shots—and the overwhelming majority of all returns of service and first volleys are hit cross-court. Thus, the smart Aussies are just playing percentages: the usual number of weak shots gives them good chances at kills, and the winners that result by far exceed the losers. Obviously, timing and deception are important, or the opponents would start playing more down-the-line shots. And so the fake drift has been invented to add further frustrations to the poor server's lot!

The drift, and all the variations of the drift, prove once again the power of the Doherty formation, which places the partner of the receiver at a modified net position.

The Draw Play

The draw play represents perfect team play at the net. It is a complex maneuver that permits the opponents to find a "safe" opening in your defenses; and they are drawn into hitting a "sure winner"— just in time for you to close the hole, cut off the shot, and slam it away for a point of your own.

There are two versions of the draw—one in which you deliberately move or remain out of position to invite an opening, the other in which your team has been forced so far out of position that a complete recovery before the opponent's next shot is impossible. The most common example of the "deliberate" draw play is a fake poach by the net man, who starts his poach too soon in order to draw a return of service down the sideline, then reverses quickly to volley deep cross-court for the point. The situation is much more complex when your team has been forced far out of position. To pull off a "desperation" draw play you have an instant—the one right instant—to start running to cut off the return hit into the gap. If you start too late, you will be unable to reach the ball; and if you start too soon, the opponents can change their shot and hit the ball behind you for an easy win. The time for decision is mighty short, but the reward for the proper answer is great: it can turn a point that has been hopelessly lost into a sensational winner. (Figures 99 and 100 illustrate the two types of draw plays.)

CHAPTER VII

Base-Line Play

In doubles points are won from the net, not from the base line. So it stands to reason that the primary objective of back-court play is to get the devil out of the back court. A team should never willingly linger in the back court; if it is forced to retreat there it must maneuver to regain the net, and once an opening is gained it should set sail for the forecourt immediately. Don't forget that the data taken at the 1952 National Doubles Championship (Table V) show that, excluding the serve and return of service (which must be played from back court), only 10 to 20 per cent of points are won from the back-court position! In club doubles the percentage runs from 15 to 30 per cent. There is no doubt about it: the base-line region should be avoided like the plague.

Once a team is pinned in the back court, getting out is by no means easy. It requires sound thinking as well as sound stroke production. And perseverance helps, too. Never stop trying, no matter how helpless the cause may appear. Remember that more errors than placements will be made by your opponents, even if they are the best of doubles players. It is remarkable how often an opponent at net will lose a point by trying, too heroically or peevishly, to murder a miraculous back-court save. If he does not lose by overhitting, he may lose by assuming the point is already won and failing to hurry back to his proper position. (An example of such a save taken from the finals of the 1954 National Doubles Championship is shown in Figure 101.) Remember also to keep all your defensive shots (other than lobs) low so that the net team cannot volley down with severity.

The proper team formation for back-court play depends, of course, upon the circumstances. The best position for receiving service is with the receiver's partner standing at a modified net position (Figure 11). In most cases he should not retreat unless forced to do so, but hold his net position in the expectation that his partner will manage to reach the net on the return of service or on a succeeding stroke. Assuming the receiver has failed to get in to the net on the return of service, there are really two basic back-court formations: the one-up, one-back; and the parallel formation with both partners back. When both partners are back, each should stand about one foot back of the base line at the mid-point of his half of the base line. Naturally, these positions should change as soon as you anticipate the direction, depth, and speed of the volley or overhead return. For example, if both players are back, one or both may edge forward a couple of steps if a drop volley is anticipated; or both players may move to the right or left on anticipating a cross-court overhead. Generally both players should move up to net together when opportunity knocks. With one up and one back, the net man may run for the base line if his partner hits an easy-to-smash weak lob, or he may move toward the center to poach if he senses that his partner's shot will force a return volley to be hit up.

So much for the basic formations. Let us now look at the strokes that are recommended.

The Dink

The dink shot family, including the soft top spin shot as well as the chopped or sliced dink, is notably effective in back-court play. Here are the reasons why:

1. The slow speed of the ball permits the striker time to follow the shot in to the net.

2. The opponents at net are usually forced to volley up, thus giving the striker a chance to make a forcing volley as he moves in to the net.

3. The soft nature of the shot ordinarily prevents the opponents from getting much pace on the return volley.

The dink shot is especially effective when played from the vicinity of the service line. From this area it can be placed with great accuracy at the feet of the opposition or into an open spot.

There are only two circumstances under which the use of the dink shot may be dangerous: (1) when the opponents are crowding the

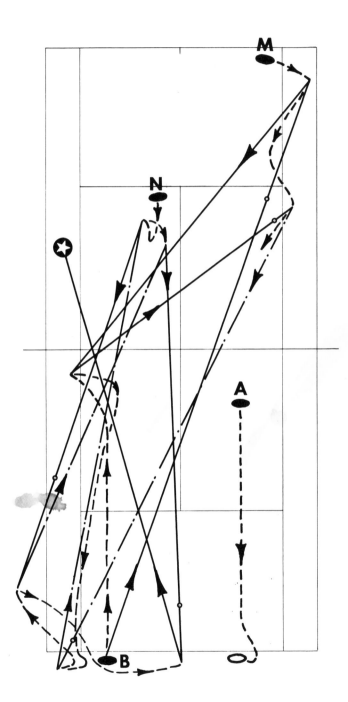

Figure 101

This diagram shows why each point should be run out, no matter how hopeless things seem. Server **B**, Seixas, makes his first volley shallow after a nice dink return of service by Rosewall, **M**. Rosewall seizes the advantage and lifts a lovely lob deep to the base line. After a hard run Seixas hits a backhand lob that Hoad, **N**, smashes at a sharp angle with tremendous power. Seixas reverses direction again and after another sprint hits a backhand lob again to Hoad. Trabert, **A**, then sets sail for the base line to attempt to cover, for Seixas is badly out of position and Hoad has the whole court open. Hoad elects to smash deep to the center. It looks as though the point is all over, and Hoad just stands his ground and watches the ball. However, Seixas pours on the coal to make his third great run; and while moving at top speed he gambles with a topped forehand angled down the sideline. It catches the astonished Hoad flat-footed and goes for a placement.

net so tightly that they may be able to angle off the return volley for a placement, and (2) when the stroke is played from so far back in the court that the opponents have time to anticipate a soft return and move in rapidly on top of the net for a sharp-angle volley. In such a situation the striker should camouflage his intention until the last moment.

The Australians have mastered a very effective back-court maneuver built around the dink. Having worked their usual one-up, one-back formation to gain the net, the man in the back court hits a low cross-court dink, forcing the opposing net player to volley up. The return volley is almost invariably hit back cross-court toward the Aussie moving in. Anticipating carefully, and timing the move to perfection, his partner at net executes a poach close to the net and volleys the ball for a placement. Net players with quick reflexes, like Sedgman, Rose, and Hoad, and with long reaches like MacGregor, are particularly adept at bringing off this beautiful play (see Figure 102).

Still another maneuver built around the dink—hereby christened the double dink—can force openings in the opposing ranks as shown in Figures 103 and 104.

The Drive

Used wisely and well, the drive is an effective weapon for back-court play.

1. It can put the ball through a hole in the formation of the opposing net team. Against the average doubles team a hole often appears down the center of the court between the two net players—a hole that fairly begs for exploitation by a hard drive from back court. Common failings create such openings. Partners are inclined to stand too far apart instead of crowding the center a bit (see Figure 26 for the proper position); and from time to time, even if they are in position, they will pull the Alphonse and Gaston act, or at least hesitate until it is too late to play the ball effectively.

2. If a team overcrowds the center, a drive can be slipped neatly down the sideline or hit on a sharp cross-court angle for a placement.

3. If the ball is played from a point deep and wide of the court, the opportunity opens up for a drive down the line to the corner (it may not even have to pass over the net), or a very sharply angled drive cross-court to open country in front of the net player.

4. A hard drive can draw errors or weak returns from sheer speed alone. A short volley landing near the service line with a fairly high

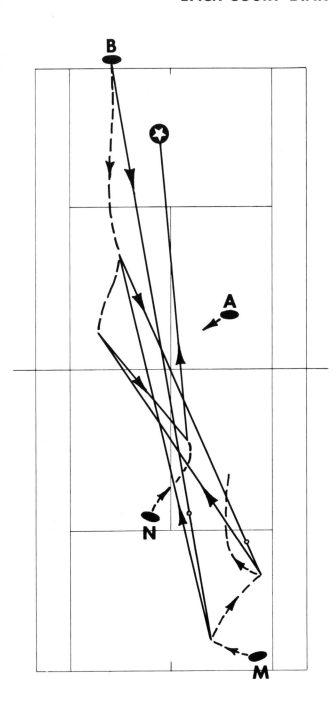

This diagram illustrates one of the favorite back-court team plays of the old fox, John Bromwich.

The serve by **B** is an excellent one and receiver **M**, Bromwich, cannot make a return of service sufficiently effective to allow him to follow the return of service in to net. Server **B** hits his first volley fairly deep cross-court and continues in to the net. But Bromwich still has some room left and manages to slip a tantalizing cross-court dink in front of **B**. This is immediately noted by modified net man **N**, Sedgman, and he gets set to cut off the return, which he knows had to be hit up by server **B**. Sedgman moves forward slightly, waits until he is certain of the direction of the return, and then rushes in to poach and slam a volley down the middle for an easy placement.

Figure 102

Once again Bromwich shows us how to engineer a service break by great back-court play.

This time receiver **M**, Bromwich, hits a dink return of service wide toward the alley. Server **B** comes in very fast and makes a good cross-court volley just beyond the service line. As Bromwich moves up to hit his ground stroke he sees that server **B** is moving toward the center, so Brom crosses him up by hitting a second and more sharply angled dink to the alley. Then he streaks for the net and, having opened a gaping hole in the defense, is able to hit the return volley down the middle for a fine point.

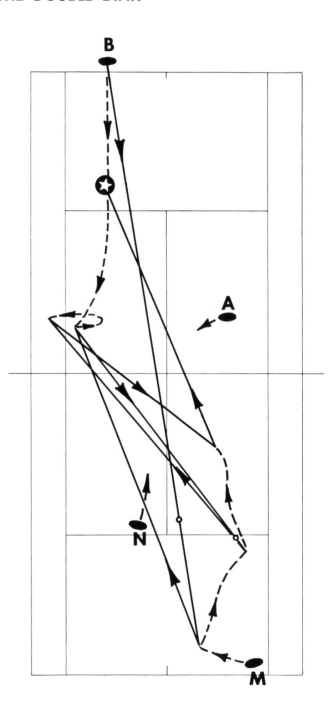

Figure 103

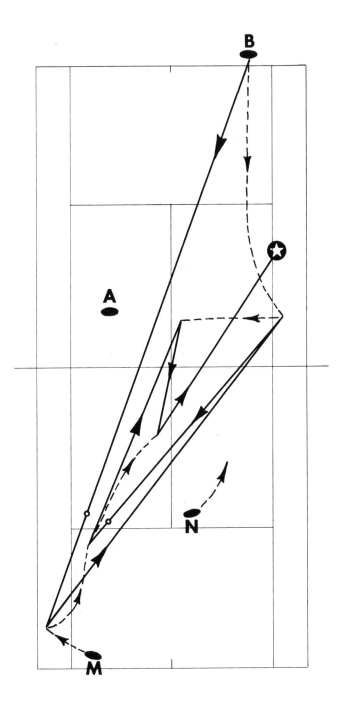

Figure 104

Here is another version of the double dink as demonstrated by Gardner Mulloy.

Receiver **M,** Mulloy, starts maneuvering for the point as did Bromwich in Figure 102. Thus the first dink on the return of service is hit wide. However, after making his first volley, server **B** is slow in covering the center. So this time Mulloy wisely decides to play his second dink to the middle, forcing server **B** to volley up from that point. Then Mulloy moves in to net very rapidly and, having drawn the opponents to the middle, angle volleys beautifully for the placement.

bounce is deadly for the net team and delightful for the driver. A hard drive from this vicinity will often win the point outright: the opponents at net have so little time to get set for the shot. To make this drive a player should study the position of the opponents up to the last second. Then he can hit toward an opening or one that is developing, instead of one that no longer exists. If the ball has a low bounce, the drive cannot be hit quite as hard. But it should at least be possible to force a weak return so that the point can be won on the next stroke. For example, in the Davis Cup Challenge Round against Australia in 1953, Seixas and Trabert used with great success a tactic suggested at the last minute: whenever they had to hit a low-bouncing ball from the service-line area against a perfectly positioned net team, they would aim driving ground strokes right at an opponent's midriff. This produced many an awkward return volley, and directly or indirectly led to many points for the Americans.

The topped drive is a useful stroke to have in your repertoire for back-court play, particularly after a shallow first volley by the server. Trabert used the stroke to cinch the Davis Cup for the United States in 1954 (see Figure 105).

From close to the base line the picture is entirely different. Except to exploit a hole in the opponent's formation, to change the pace, or to draw a weak return, the drive is a foolish shot to play. An alert, properly positioned net team can usually volley the best base-line drives back deep with devastating speed, and can angle them off for placements (see Figure 106) from close to the net. Furthermore, the speed of the drive does not give the striker time to move well in toward the net, so his chances of ultimately gaining the point are slim. If a well-concealed drive does, fortunately, draw a short return volley, it is often best to play a dink on the next shot. It will force the opponents to volley up and to give the striker, and if necessary his partner, plenty of time to complete the journey to the net. Such dinks can be played effectively in the center or at the feet of the opponents.

A warning on improper use of the drive from the base line. When your partner is in the modified net position—the one-up, one-back defensive formation—do *not* play a drive down the line. The reason is quite obvious: in this spot the drive hands the opposing net man a wonderful cross-court shot through the familiar open diagonal for a placement. (See Figure 107.)

But like most rules this "don't" has exceptions: the down-the-line shot *is* recommended when the net man has left a hole along the side line (see Figure 108), and when the net man starts a poach prema-

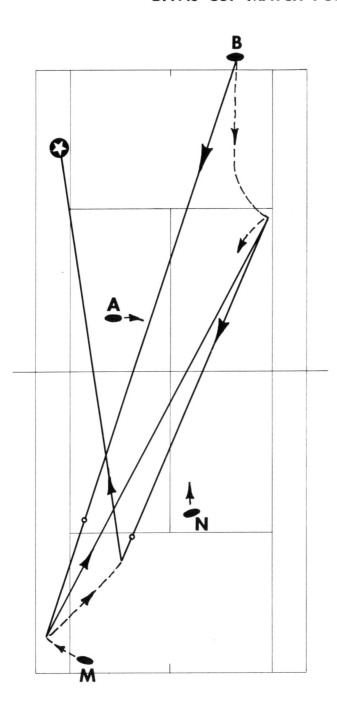

Figure 105

This point shows Trabert using a topped drive to win the Davis Cup.

On match point Rosewall, **B**, serves and Trabert, **M**, moves in and returns a topped backhand drive quickly at Rosewall's feet. This forces Rosewall to volley short to a point near the middle just beyond the service line. Trabert, moving in on his return, decides to play the ball on the bounce. In noting the last-second actions of the opponents, he sees Hoad, **A**, edging toward the center. So Trabert sets his feet and body to fake a routine cross-court return to Rosewall. Then, at the last moment, he rolls a lovely topped forehand drive down the alley past the astonished Hoad for the point, set, match, and Davis Cup!

This may have been a gag, but it illustrates the point. Receiver **M** is none other than Pancho Segura, whose two-fisted forehand drive is one of the hardest in tennis. So he decides to see if he can drive one through the net man, who happens to be the other Pancho, Gonzales. Segura hits three scorchers as hard as he can at Gonzales, **A.** The poor tactics are obvious. Since Segura is deep, Gonzales has plenty of time to get set for each shot. He merely works Segura, **M,** toward the center and then moves in and angle volleys for the point.

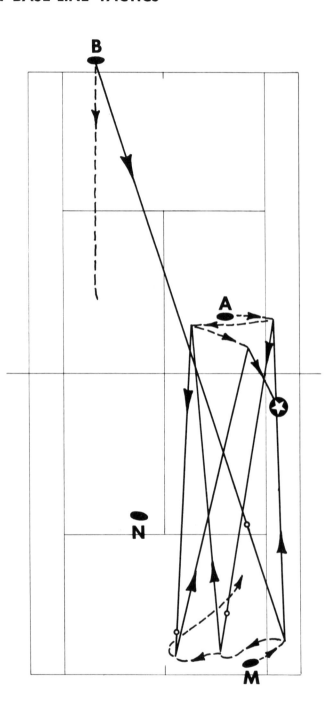

Figure 106

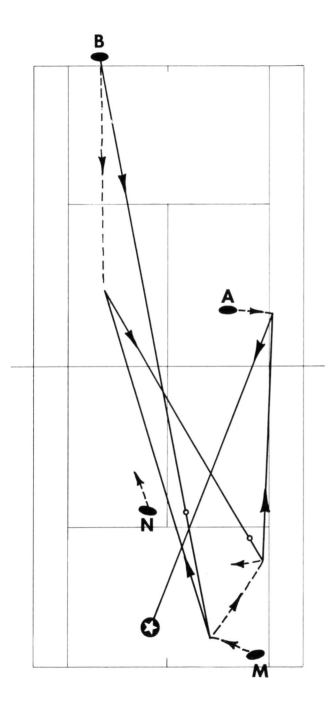

Receiver **M** takes a bad gamble on this play. By trying to drive the server's first volley down the line instead of cross-court, he gives the net man a high ball (high because it has to go over the highest part of the net). Furthermore, all that net man **A** has to do to win the point is slap a sharp backhand cross-court volley through the open diagonal for the point. You have to catch net man **A** asleep or surprise him to make this gamble worthwhile (see Figure 108).

Figure 107

turely and can be caught moving in the wrong direction (see Figure 110).

The Lob

The lob is the best shot to use from the back court under these circumstances:

1. A high, defensive lob is a wise tactic when the return is played from a point very deep in the court or when the striker is maneuvered way out of position by a forcing shot. It permits a team time to regain the best offensive formation before the return is made (even to the extent of allowing your partner to drop back from the net to the base line if necessary). Note the word *high*. So often in this situation a low lob is mistakenly played, and is banged away for a placement before the defensive team can return to position.

2. When one or both of the opponents are crowding the net, a low, offensive type of lob will often permit the defensive team to regain the net. The offensive lob is particularly effective from the vicinity of the service line and is used extensively from this area. In executing such a shot, remember to make the lob deep. Probably the worst play in tennis, and the best way to be murdered legally, is to lob short and run to the net. The great Tilden once knocked an opponent unconscious with a smashing answer to such a play.

3. The lob is a dandy device for catching the opponents off balance. It was this use of the lob at which Lott excelled. His offensive top-spin lob after faking a drive often caught the opposition flat-footed and bounded away toward the backstop for a placement.

It is always best, under any of these circumstances, to place the lob on the backhand side of the opposition. Very few tennis players have the ability to hit a forceful backhand overhead. Thus, a well-placed lob can oftimes save a point, even if the trajectory is too low. In fact, Talbert often purposely lobs a bit low in such a way as to force the net man to move back just a couple of steps to hit a high backhand volley. Then he moves rapidly in to volley offensively the return.

The wind and sun are also important considerations in executing a lob. In warming up for a match, take careful note of the strength and direction of both wind and sun. Since the height, strength, and direction of the lob may have to be altered materially with a change of courts between games, a mental lapse can cause a high lob hit thoughtlessly down the wrong sideline to be blown off court, or a lob hit carelessly into the wind to hang and be killed easily by an angled overhead.

(Mental lapses are inexcusable in championship tennis and embarrassing to the week-ender.) The wind makes lobbing more difficult, but it also makes overhead smashes much harder to time properly; so lobbing should by no means be ruled out on a windy day. It may appear unsportsmanlike, but it is nevertheless sound tactics to use the lob more often when the opposing net team is facing the sun. Just as it makes sense in singles to run an older or heavier opponent on a hot day, so in doubles it is downright practical to lob toward the sun and concentrate on the shorter opponent with the weaker overhead. Bitsy Grant never complained although he was lobbed to death in championship doubles.

As men grow taller and overhead play becomes more devastating, the lob in doubles is rapidly becoming a shot that should be played only as a purely defensive measure, or offensively when hidden by a clever fake up to the last moment. It is doubtful whether a team specializing in the lob, as the famous Kinsey brothers did, will ever reach tennis greatness again.

(Offensive and defensive lobs are illustrated in Figures 108 through 110.)

Miscellaneous

Once in a while a mixup occurs during the progress of a point, and three or four of the players turn up in the back court. In playing a ball from the base line in this situation, a shot Bitsy Grant called a half-lob is recommended—a high soft drive out of reach of the net man (if there is one), which is deep and floats long enough to permit the striker's team to gain the net. A fast drive under such circumstances often boomerangs, as it allows the opponent to return the ball at the feet of the inrushing team, forcing them to half-volley or volley up defensively.

Some of the most complex and splendid defensive team plays occur when the receiver is pinned in the back court with his partner at the modified net or net position. The play can be triggered by the modified net man or by the receiver, depending on the circumstances. In either event it requires split-second thinking and a complete understanding between partners. When triggered by the modified net player it is dubbed the "let-go-by" play (see Figure 25). Suppose a hard volley is hit down the middle within possible reach of the modified net player. Instantaneously he must judge whether he or his partner will have the better chance to return the ball effectively. Each partner must know

Receiver **M** gives a fine exhibition of defensive lobbing in this point. Server **B** slices a serve to the forehand, which forces receiver **M** to make the return while scrambling hard. So **M** elects to hit a defensive lob down the line. He keeps the ball high and deep to give himself time to get back into position and to prevent net man **A** from getting sufficient angle on his overhead to put it away easily. Net man **A** has to hit the overhead from back of the service line, so he decides to play it down the middle. Receiver **M** is now back in position, and as he gets set to play the shot he sees net man **A** moving back into net, so **M** hits another deep defensive lob. This time net man **A** plays his overhead a bit shallow. As receiver **M** moves up he notes that net man **A** is slow in returning to his net position. Therefore, **M** wallops a hard drive down the line for a well-earned point.

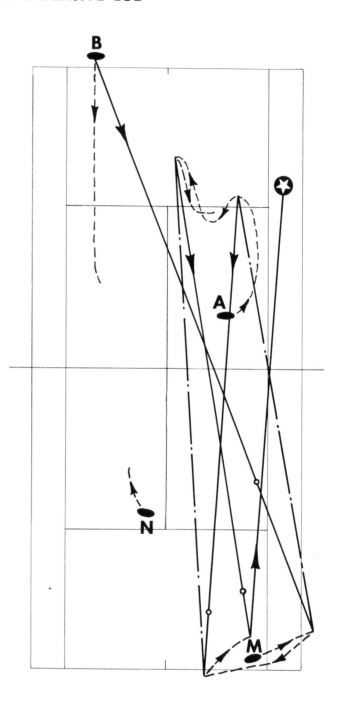

Figure 108

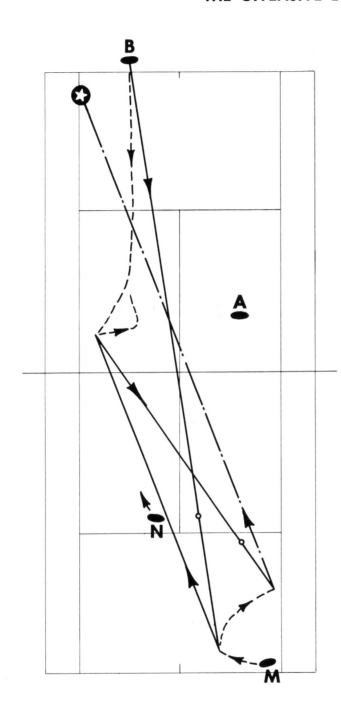

Figure 109

Here is a perfect example of the offensive lob made famous by George Lott. This point was actually played by Seixas who possesses a top-spin lob similar to Lott's.

Receiver **M**, Seixas, returns service with a low cross-court dink that pulls server **B** way in to the net and forces him to volley up cross-court. As Seixas moves up he sees that he has a perfect setup for an offensive lob: the server's first volley is short, so the stroke can be played from near the service line; server **B** has been forced in too close to the net; and it is possible to take advantage of maximum distance by playing diagonally to the farthest corner of the court. So, after first faking a routine cross-court drive, Seixas strokes a low, top-spin lob deep to the corner that bounds away for an easy placement.

This diagram shows a rapid shift in plans to take advantage of an opening. Receiver **M** has moved in to play the first volley of server **B** from near the service line. Receiver **M** is all set to play a cross-court ground stroke near the middle when he sees net man **A** start to drift over to intercept the shot. So at the last moment he changes plans and hits a low lob down the line just out of reach of **A** for the point. This shot is not too bad a gamble because net man **A** would have to play a weak backhand overhead if he is able to scramble back in time to reach the ball.

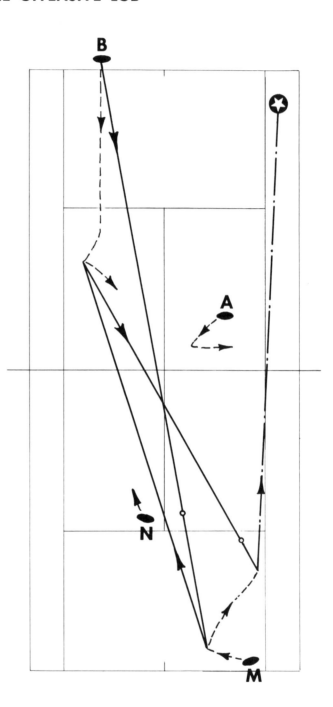

Figure 110

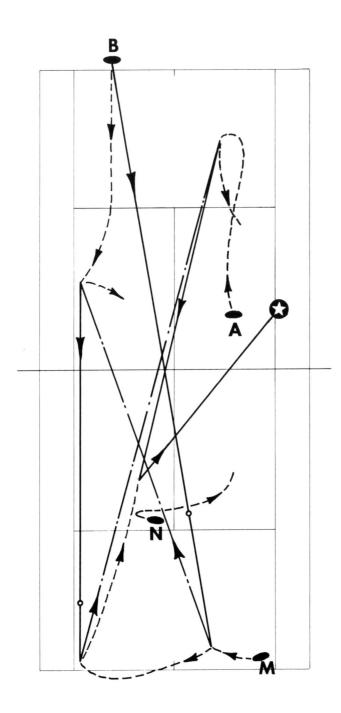

Figure 111

This point has had a bad beginning but is pulled out of the fire by brilliant team play.

Server **B** places a scorching flat serve in the corner and almost aces receiver **M**. In fact all that **M** can do is hit a poor defensive lob, which is a sitting duck. Server **B** comes in and sets himself for a routine overhead down the line past modified net man **N** for an easy point. As modified net man **N** moves to cover the shot, receiver **M** sees that the chances are much better for him to retrieve the ball. So receiver **M** yells "Mine," and rushes to his left as soon as server **B** is committed to his down-the-line shot. As **M** runs to cover and hits a deep, high, defensive cross-court lob, player **N** crosses over to the unprotected side. The lob is so well played that net man **A** is forced to hit it from way back of the service line. This gives receiver **M** his second chance to make a beautiful play. He anticipates that net man **A** will play a weak, off-balance overhead down the center, pauses until **A** is fully committed, dashes forward at top speed, and makes a gorgeous backhand angle volley return of the smash to win a hair-raising point.

what the other will and can do under such circumstances; else the ball may sail through for a placement. The play can be triggered by the back-court player if he anticipates that he will have a better shot at a ball about to be slammed at the net player. He calls for the ball by saying, "Mine," and crosses over to cover behind his partner. Such a play is shown in Figure 111. Defensive back-court team play of this advanced caliber is not only beautiful to watch; it is heartbreaking to play against.

CHAPTER VIII

Summary

There are those who say, "Tennis is just fun, a sport—why try to make it into a science?" Secretly these people know the answer to their own question: doubles is a competitive game, and in any kind of competition it is more fun to win than to lose. The urge to excel is so basic that even the most casual and occasional player, who loftily disclaims any real interest in the game, is continually (and sometimes unconsciously) trying to strengthen his backhand, diagnose his opponent's tactics, or put more stuff into his serve. So the "scientific" side of doubles offers something for everyone who has ever lifted a racquet. To the casual player it offers the increased satisfaction that comes with playing better. To the more regular player or interested novice it offers a general concept of court strategy and all-around play—his game is bound to improve as he grasps the principles behind sound maneuvers. To the expert, seasoned amateur or gifted pro, it offers more than just a review of essentials—it represents a challenge for him to apply the concentrated thought, study, and practice required to bring his game to the top and to develop new and better variations. And to the ardent spectator, the tennis wife, or the tired businessman enjoying an afternoon in the sun, it offers a sense of participation—the added pleasure and excitement of appreciating the finer points of the tactics used—of being "in the know." We remember once many years ago sitting with a Davis Cup singles player at Forest Hills as he was watching George Lott play in a Davis Cup doubles match. While we watched sober and unappreciating, our friend was having trouble maintaining a respectful silence—he was doubled up with amusement as he watched

207

Lott make monkeys of the other team with his wonderful dinks and fakes. Yes, you will get out of the game exactly what you put into it.

It is well-nigh impossible to summarize effectively a game like doubles, which is composed of an enormous number of factors, each of significant and independent importance. However, here, by way of review, are some of the salient features.

The object of the game is to win; but to win graciously within the framework of good sportsmanship. The time to start winning is at the outset—beginning with the very first point. If you can get the jump and forge ahead, you put the pressure on the opponents, and you can afford to gamble more often. Once you have built up a lead, do not let down—the fortunes can turn against you with lightning speed if you slow your pace even imperceptibly. There are no half-measures: if you are not on the attack, you are automatically on the defensive.

The first step toward playing doubles is to form a team. Now a team is a lot more than two players on the same side of the net. It is a combination of two players having complementary games (that is, a playmaker and a put-away artist) and a healthy respect for each other. Once the partners are chosen, they should work on coordinating offensive and defensive team play for at least two or three years. It takes that much planning, practicing, playing, and discussing doubles for two players to "jell" into a team, to develop the habit of thinking and acting as one in every situation. (For some obscure reason the United States used doubles "teams" without team experience in the 1950, 1951, and 1952 Davis Cup Challenge Rounds; and the Australians tried the same thing in 1953. In all four cases the unseasoned team lost. Future team selectors might take note.) Teamwork counts for about 25 per cent of successful doubles play.

To be a winning combination a team must realize that points are scored as much by the head as by the racquet. Continued concentration is required. Mental lapses make for lost points. Sound tactics and teamwork, coupled with a wide repertoire of solid strokes, are the hallmarks of a successful doubles combine. Teamwork includes a steady exchange of encouragement between partners—good team morale will win points and also save points by steadying the unsettled player. And teamwork includes the vital business of diagnosing the opponents' game.

Even the tournament player may have a stroke weakness or a tactical court-position weakness or both. A stroke weakness should be exploited by playing it but not by overplaying it. Remember that any weak stroke may become a strong weapon if you force the opponent to use it too much and thus promote his confidence in the stroke. Also a court-position weakness should be cashed in when needed, not exploited to excess. Note carefully whether the opposing net man is too close to the net, or whether he leaves the alley or center unguarded; whether the opponents fail to move to the proper defensive position against sharp cross-court return possibilities; and whether returns of service are followed in to the net. Once you have spotted such lapses you can capitalize on them for a number of crucial points.

As the quality of your game improves, the ability to anticipate becomes of vital importance. To develop this skill requires study of the style, court position, tactics, habits, and special shots of the opponents. Couple this with careful notation of the position of the opponents' racquet arm, feet, and backswing, and you should be able to anticipate the direction, speed, and type of shot about to be played. You will begin to find yourself in the right spot at the right time—ready and waiting for the return. Ability to anticipate is the big difference between the mediocre and the good doubles player, and great anticipation is the key to impossible saves and delicate strategems of the masters—the Lotts, Bromwiches, and Brugnons. But once learned, don't for a moment believe that anticipation and game analysis are your wholly owned secret formula for success at doubles: your opponents are anticipating and analyzing too; and to win you must match them stroke for stroke, cover the court as well as they do, and *then* outthink and outmaneuver them in the bargain.

So much for basic matters. Now for a capsule review of pointers on service, return of service, net play, and back court play.

The service has been called the one most important stroke in doubles. If they can't break your serve, they can't beat you! The serving team has an offensive advantage that must be clung to tenaciously. About 30 per cent of all strokes used in doubles, and 20 per cent of all winning shots are serves. Losing the offensive advantage and dropping a service game is one of the cardinal sins of doubles. One loss of service often results in the loss of a set: newspaper accounts of doubles matches emphasize the service breaks more than any other single item. To make capital of the service, the stroke should force a defensive return by the receiver and permit the server to get within about fifteen feet of the net as he follows his service in to the volley position. For both purposes it is best to develop a dependable American twist service that will put the *first ball* into play about 80 per cent of the time (the server has almost twice as good a chance to win the point with a good first service as with a good second service). The preferred target for the service is deep in the receiver's backhand corner. The twist serve should be hit about three-fourths speed to give the server control and plenty of time to get on top of the net so that he can volley the return of service down offensively. Other types, speeds, and targets of service should be used sparingly, and then just to keep the receiver guessing and to prevent him from taking liberties. If you are prone to disregard the percentages and make a big noise with a cannonball serve, just remember that in doubles as fine a server as Kramer holds his cannonball in reserve and relies almost entirely on his American twist.

The partner of the server at net must note the bounce point of the service, watch the receiver in order to anticipate the type and direction of the return of service, and then move to the proper spot to establish the best offensive formation. In general his move will be toward the center of the court. He should be prepared to poach to put away weak returns of service, and to move fast to cover effective offensive lob returns even when hit over the advancing server's head. The net man also plays an important part in any of the numerous variations of the reverse service formations and the signaled poach plays.

The return of service is the most difficult shot in doubles. This is apparent when you realize that this stroke sets the stage for the receiving team, which team loses twice as many points as it wins. Actually 20 per cent of all attempted returns of service end up in errors, and only 12 per cent result in winners, a mere handful of which are placements.

The receiving team must get as close to an attacking position as possible. The partner of the receiver should be at a modified net position just inside the service line near the center of the court. The receiver himself should be a step or more inside the base line for a first service. Every step that it is safe to move in against the particular server is an advantage, as it gives the receiver a better chance to take the serve earlier, return it offensively at the feet of the incoming server, and rush to the attacking position at net in the minimum elapsed time.

If the receiver can make a very effective return of service *and* get well in to the net, he switches the odds on winning the point from two-to-one against him to two-to-one in his favor. The job can best be done by playing a slow, low, cross-court return out of reach of the opposing net man: a sharply angled, soft, spinning dink shot or topped drive well inside the opponent's service line will force the server to volley up and give the receiving team the time they need to reach the attacking position at net. Also this type of service return, which might better be named an approach shot, cannot be volleyed down or through the receiver's partner. To keep the server and net man guessing, an occasional flat drive cross-court or down the line or a lob should be played by the receiver. But above all the receiver must somehow manage to get the ball back over the net, and thus force the serving team to *win* the point: remember, the very best of doubles players make twice as many errors as placements—some on the feeblest of returns. So just by avoiding the outright loss of the point on the return of service, the receiving team assures itself an almost even chance of winning the point.

The partner of the receiver at the modified net position must develop the habit of carrying out the following sequence: watch the type of return being made by the receiver; then the actions of the opposing net man; and, if the ball gets safely past the net man, he must watch the advancing server in order to have a chance of anticipating and returning a ball volleyed sharply at him from close range by either opponent. He should also be ready to put away weak first volleys hit within his reach. Since most first volleys are hit cross-court by the server, the partner of the receiver usually finds it profitable to drift forward and toward the center on such volleys. He will be able to cut off many of these with crisp volleys, and will also force the server to err trying to keep the ball away from him. Thus an alert modified net man should make his share of placements and "impossible" saves.

The receiver and his partner face the problem of turning odds of about seven-to-one against them into a successful service break. By using the most effective kinds of service return, by following the return well in toward the net, by cashing in the offensive moves of the modified net man, by employing ingenious and varying tactics to steal the offensive from the serving team, and by hanging in there under all kinds of pressure, the receiving team can frequently turn the tide.

Net play is the thing that wins doubles matches. Remember that one-third of all shots in doubles are volleys; and excluding the service and return of service, which must be played from the back court, a staggering 80 per cent of all points are won at the net position. And 80 per cent of all placements are made from the net position.

Net play starts with the first volley, the most important and most difficult volley, of which about 85 per cent are made by the server as he advances to the net position. The server must play this volley effectively if he is to win his service. If the return of service is high, the server must be in far enough to hit down for a placement, or at least to force a weak return that will lead to a winner on the next volley. If the return is weak enough to permit a poach, the net man should be able to knock it away for a point. Usually the server and the poacher drive weak returns at or past the opponent in the modified net position. On the other hand, if the return of service is so expertly executed as to force the server to hit up a weak volley, the receiving team should be able to move in quickly and volley down for the winner.

In almost half the cases there is no immediate winner; an intermediate situation prevails and the net position battle is joined. The server should generally play his first volley deep down the middle if the receiver hangs back, or at his feet near the middle if he advances. Then begins the struggle to jockey the opponents out of position or to force a weak return. Standard strategy calls for crisp volleys to the center to draw the opponents to the middle, then an angle volley for the point; or angle volleys to open up the center for an unanswerable volley deep down the middle. A soft volley at the feet of the opposition will often force a volley or half-volley up, so that the striking team can move in on top of the net and volley down heavily to win the point. The net battle is so fast that good anticipation is a must.

In every phase of doubles, but especially in the "kills" of net play, touch is an indispensable ingredient in your game. It is touch, the absolute balance and aptness of shot-making, that enables you to put the ball away with finality: overhitting leads to errors; underhitting leads to unexpected "gets" by the opponents, often resulting in lost points. Part of touch is adjusting put-away strokes to the speed of the opposition and of the playing surface. A rule of thumb: the faster the court the softer the put-away shot; the faster the opposition, the harder the shot.

In good doubles there is almost no base-line play: a player never remains on, or retreats to, the base line unless he is forced to do so. If you find yourself marooned in the back court you should mix up well-concealed low dinks and drives with lobs—anything to get back toward the net safely and at once. If your partner is at net, do not play down the line, except as a surprise play; it usually hands the opponents a fine opportunity for a placement in the open diagonal. Do not lob short—your partner may be mortally wounded by an overhead smash. And in case you forget, let every second you spend in the back court remind you that only 20 per cent of the points in doubles (exclusive of service and return of service) are won from way back yonder in the cornfield.

No matter how bleak the outlook during a point, don't give up the ship! Figure 112 shows the way the masters fight for a point.

Well, what does it all add up to? The answer, in a word, is court-craft. By courtcraft we mean selecting the proper shot, placing it strategically, and positioning yourself and partner in the best manner

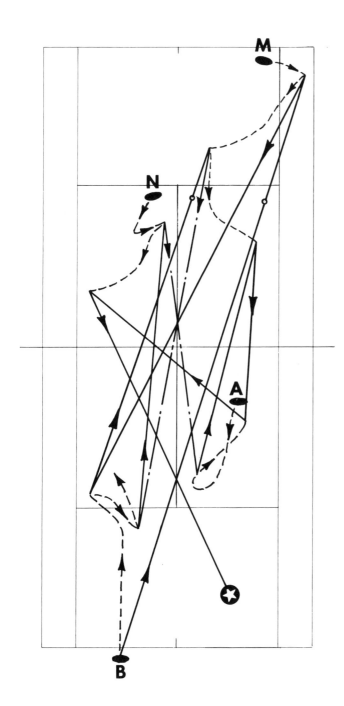

Figure 112

This play shows how, by pure fight and determination, a thrice-lost point can be won from even the best of players.

Server Kramer, **B,** plays a fine first volley low to the middle, which receiver Sedgman, **M,** decides to play as a ground stroke. Sedgman lobs, but not deep enough, and the point appears lost as Kramer moves back and hits a tremendous overhead smash. However, modified net man McGregor, **N,** is watching carefully and is rewarded by being able to stick out his racquet at the last second and save the point temporarily with a weak, high lob volley return. Net man Segura, **A,** drops back and powders a second overhead down the line for a second apparent winner. But Sedgman, **M,** is in no mood to give up the ship. He moves over rapidly and just manages to return a weak volley. Segura is almost smiling cockily at this moment as he moves in for a sure winner this time—the cross-court angle volley area is wide open. But as Segura, **A,** makes the shot, McGregor anticipates beautifully and roars in to blast a deep volley between Kramer and Segura for an incredible point!

to deal with any return: it is a developed instinct for good doubles that guides you to the correct tactical maneuver under the tremendous variety of circumstances you will inevitably face. Once the basic principles are mastered, you can devote yourself to polishing your strokes, perfecting your team play; sharpening your anticipation, increasing your consistency—and getting even greater enjoyment out of the great game of doubles.